Judetinnemore

COLLINS GEM

november, 1997.

BOOK OF PRAYERS

Compiled
Robert Van de

(from Christchu Priory)

HarperCollins*Publishers*

D1390435

HarperCollins Publishers
P. O. Box, Glasgow G4 0NB

First published 1994

Reprint 9 8 7 6 5 4 3 2 1 0

ISBN 0 00 470555 6

The Collins Gem *Book of Prayers* is based on material
contained in *The Fount Book of Prayer* by Robert Van de
Weyer, first published by HarperCollins Publishers in 1993

Printed in Italy by Amadeus S.p.A., Rome

Contents

God's care

The human condition

The person of Jesus

Introduction

Praying is having a conversation with God. Jesus Christ teaches us that we should regard God as our Father, and speak to him with the same intimacy that we talk to our natural parents. And other religions have discovered this same closeness to God. Of course in human terms it is a one-way conversation, since God rarely, if ever answers our prayers in words. But people in all ages have sensed that God listens, and that he replies through intimations and events.

There is no special art or skill to prayer. When the disciples asked Jesus to teach them to pray he gave them a series of phrases, that we now call the Lord's Prayer - which simply express the various attitudes and emotions that can prompt prayer: praise, gratitude, petitions, repentance. And on numerous occasions he told them to turn to God at any moment of the day, for every need. Later Paul urged people 'to pray without ceasing', so that at work and at rest their hearts and minds would be constantly open to God. Over the centuries many special prayers have been written, often of great beauty and elegance, to be recited in public worship. Yet in essence prayer is natural and spontaneous, and, above all, personal.

In our ordinary conversations with friends we often pick up phrases and idioms, and even styles of communications, which we can use ourselves; and as small children we have to learn speech itself. In the same way in our relationship with God, it can be helpful to eavesdrop on other people talking to God, to pick up hints on how to express ourselves more fully. And at times of major crisis we can sometimes find ourselves unable to put our feelings into words, so the prayers of others can become our own.

This book is a collection of spiritual eavesdropping. Very few of the prayers contained here were composed for public use, or indeed were ever intended to be read by others. Rather they are largely taken from private devotional writings, which in many cases were only found and published after the author's death. Some of the great spiritual guides only wrote about God, and never put their own prayers on paper. But happily in most of the great spiritual classics the authors from time to time turn directly to God, giving a direct insight into this relationship with God. So most of the famous names from our spiritual history are included here, as well as some lesser-known figures.

Jesus laid particular emphasis on talking to God, so inevitably most of the prayers here are Christian. But many people of other faiths, including tribal religions, have enjoyed the same intimacy of spiritual communication; so Muslims, Hindus, Buddhists and Sikhs, as well as various tribes, are also represented. If the book teaches anything, it is that one's method of prayer does not depend on religion or culture, but on temperament and circumstance. A Spanish man in the sixteenth century may pray in much the same way as a Hindu prince two millennia earlier; the prayer of a German pastor, about to be executed by the Nazis, may echo the words of a third century bishop fearful of persecution.

The prayers are arranged according to themes, to help the reader find words suitable for their own emotions and situation. But personal prayers of this kind rarely slip neatly into categories, so it is often a matter of finding prayers that fit one's own natural style of communication. At all events the book is intended as a kind of spiritual well, to be dipped into at will.

Most of the prayers here were not written in English. In translating them, modern English has been used. Those prayers which were composed in English are given in their original form, which is some cases is quite archaic. But all the prayers are easily intelligible.

Robert Van de Weyer

Through
the day

WAKING

Jesus, a look from you can draw us from our slumbers, and set us firmly on our feet. Sin shudders and falters at your glance, and guilt dissolves into tears of repentance. Shine, then, on our torpid minds and set our dormant thoughts astir. May we leave sin behind us, and may our first action be to turn to you in repentant prayer.

Ambrose of Milan

Living Lord, you have watched over me, and put your hand on my head, during the long, dark hours of night. Your holy angels have protected me from all harm and pain. To you, Lord, I owe life itself. Continue to watch over me and bless me during the hours of day.

Jacob Boehme

My God, Father and Preserver, who in your goodness has watched over me in this past night and brought me to this day, grant that I may spend the day wholly in your service.

Let me not think or say or do a single thing
that is not in obedience to your will; but
rather let all my actions be directed to your
glory and the salvation of my brethren. Let
me attempt nothing that is not pleasing to
you; but rather let me seek happiness only in
your grace and goodness. Grant also that as I
labour for the goods and clothing necessary
for this life, I may constantly raise my mind
upwards to the heavenly life which you
promise to all your children.

John Calvin

Lord Jesus Christ, you are the sun that
always rises, but never sets. You are the
source of all life, creating and sustaining
every living thing. You are the source of all
food, material and spiritual, nourishing us in
both body and soul. You are the light that
dispels the clouds of error and doubt, and
goes before me every hour of the day,
guiding my thoughts and my actions. May I
walk in your light, be nourished by your
food, be sustained by your mercy, and be
warmed by your love.

Erasmus

WORKING

Give me, dear Lord, a pure heart and a wise mind, that I may carry out my work according to your will. Save me from all false desires, from pride, greed, envy and anger, and let me accept joyfully every task you set before me. Let me seek to serve the poor, the sad and those unable to work. Help me to discern honestly my own gifts that I may do the things of which I am capable, and happily and humbly leave the rest to others. Above all, remind me constantly that I have nothing except what you give me, and can do nothing except what you enable me to do.

Jacob Boehme

My God, Father and Saviour, since you have commanded us to work in order to meet our needs, sanctify our labour that it may bring nourishment of our souls as well as to our bodies. Make us constantly aware that our efforts are worthless unless guided by your light and strengthened by your hand. Make us faithful to the particular tasks for which you have bestowed upon us the necessary gifts, taking from us any envy or jealousy at the vocations of others.

Give us a good heart to supply the needs of the poor, saving us from any desire to exalt ourselves over those who receive our bounty. And if you should call us into greater poverty than we humanly desire, save us from any spirit of defiance or resentment, but rather let us graciously and humbly receive the bounty of others. Above all may every temporal grace be matched by spiritual grace, that in both body and soul we may live to your glory.

John Calvin

My God, you are always close to me. In obedience to you, I must now apply myself to outward things. Yet, as I do so, I pray that you will give me the grace of your presence. And to this end I ask that you will assist my work, receive its fruits as an offering to you, and all the while direct all my affections to you.

Brother Lawrence

EATING

Lord Christ, we ask you to spread our table
with your mercy. And may you bless with
your gentle hands the good things you have
given us. We know that whatever we have
comes from your lavish heart, for all that is
good comes from you. Thus whenever we
eat, we should give thanks to you. And
having received from your hands, let us give
with equally generous hands to those who
are poor, breaking bread and sharing our
bread with them. For you have told us that
whatever we give to the poor, we give to
you.

Alcuin of York

Most gracious God, who hast given us
Christ and with him all that is necessary to
life and godliness: we thankfully take this
our food as the gift of thy bounty, procured
by his merits. Bless it to the nourishment
and strength of our frail bodies to fit us for
thy cheerful service.

Richard Baxter

O heavenly Father, which art the fountain and full treasure of all goodness, we beseech thee to show thy mercies upon us thy children, and sanctify these gifts which we receive of thy merciful liberality, granting us grace to use them soberly and purely, according to thy blessed will; so that hereby we may acknowledge thee to be the author and giver of all good things; and, above all, that may we remember continually to seek the spiritual food of thy word, wherewith our souls may be nourished everlastingly through our Saviour Christ.

John Knox

RESTING

Jesus, a look from you can embrace us with peaceful sleep, and ensure that our dreams are pure and holy. Sin shudders and falters at your glance, and guilt dissolves into tears of repentance. Bring peace, Lord, to our weary minds, and give rest to our tired limbs. May we leave sin behind us, and may our final reflections before sleep be prayers for your mercy.

Ambrose of Milan

As I take off my dusty, dirty clothes let me also be stripped of the sins I have committed this day. I confess, dear Lord, that in so many ways my thoughts and actions have been impure. Now I come before you, naked in body and bare in soul, to be washed clean. Let me rest tonight in your arms, and so may the dreams that pass through my mind be holy. And let me awake tomorrow, strong and eager to serve you.

Jacob Boehme

Now that the sun has set,
I sit and rest, and think of you.
Give my weary body peace.
Let my legs and arms stop aching,
Let my nose stop sneezing,
Let my head stop thinking.
Let me sleep in your arms.

Dinka

Lord Jesus Christ, you are the gentle moon
and joyful stars, that watch over the darkest
night. You are the source of all peace,
reconciling the whole universe to the Father.
You are the source of all rest, calming
troubled hearts, and bringing sleep to weary
bodies. You are the sweetness that fills our
minds with quiet joy, and can turn the worst
nightmares into dreams of heaven. May I
dream of your sweetness, rest in your arms,
be at one with your Father, and be
comforted in the knowledge that you always
watch over me.

Erasmus

Through
the year

ADVENT

Come now, high king of heaven. Come to us in
flesh and bone. Bring life to us who are weary
with misery. Bring peace to us who are overcome with weeping, whose cheeks are covered
with bitter salt tears. Seek us out, who are lost
in the darkness of depression. Do not forget us,
but show mercy on us. Impart to us your
everlasting joy, so that we, who are fashioned
by your hands, may praise your glory.

The Exeter Book

Stir up our hearts, we beseech you, to
prepare ourselves to receive your Son. When
he comes and knocks, may he find us not
sleeping in sin, but awake to righteousness,
ceaselessly rejoicing in his love. May our
hearts and minds be so purified, that we
may be ready to receive his promise of
eternal life.

The Gelasian Sacramentary

Lord Jesus
Help me to welcome you this Christmas

not in the cold manger of my heart,
but in a heart full of love and
humility, a heart warm with love for
others.

Mother Teresa

CHRISTMAS

What is this jewel that is so precious? I can see it has been quarried not by men, but by God.

It is you, dear Jesus. You have been dug from the rocks of Heaven itself to be offered to me as a gift beyond price.

You shine in the darkness. Every colour of the rainbow can be seen within you. The whole earth is bathed in your light.

Infant Jesus, by being born as man you have taken upon yourself the pain of death. But such a jewel can never be destroyed.

Adam of St Victor

O Lord, our King and our Saviour! Let us celebrate this festival without false ideas, but with our hearts open to receive your Word, your promise, your commandment. Our grumbles and doubts, our errors and mistakes, our stubbornness and defiance, should trouble us even during these days of joy, because they trouble you. But as we rejoice at your birth in the world, we ask you

to accept us and uplift us as we are. And we
pray that, in your strength, we shall be
willing to be counted amongst the poor and
the humble, as you counted yourself.

So we remember before you all our
brothers and sisters who are troubled and
confused, who are sick in body or in mind,
who lack the material means of survival.
And we trust that in you the Gospel of
freedom may be proclaimed more cheerfully
and joyfully by both Catholics and
Protestants alike, that they become the salt
for which the world longs. And now may we
have a good Christmas. Let us look forward
beyond the bright lights of our Christmas
decorations towards the dawning of your
eternal light.

Karl Barth

Let your goodness, Lord, appear to us, that
we, made in your image, conform ourselves
to it. In our own strength we cannot imitate
your majesty, power and wonder; nor is it
fitting for us to try. But your mercy reaches
from the heavens, through the clouds, to the

earth below. You have come to us a small
child, but you have brought us the greatest
of all gifts, the gift of eternal love. Caress us
with your tiny hands, embrace us with your
tiny arms, and pierce our hearts with your
soft, sweet cries.

Bernard of Clairvaux

Moonless darkness stands between.
Past, the Past, no more be seen!
But the Bethlehem-star may lead me
To the sight of him who freed me
From the self that I have been.
Make me pure, Lord: thou art holy;
Make me meek, Lord: thou wert lowly;
Now beginning, and alway:
Now begin, on Christmas day.

Gerard Manley Hopkins

Good Jesu, born as at this time,
A little child for love of us;
Be thou born in me, that I may
Be a little child in love of thee;
And hang on thy love as on my
Mother's bosom,

Trustfully, lovingly, peacefully;
Hushing all my cares in love of thee.

Good Jesu, sweeten every thought of mine
With the sweetness of thy love.
Good Jesu, give me a deep love for thee,
That nothing may be too hard for me
To bear for love of thee.

E.B. Pusey

LENT AND HOLY WEEK

Let me hold fast to you, beautiful Lord, whom the angels themselves yearn to look upon. Wherever you go, I will follow you. If you pass through fire, I will not flinch, I fear no evil when you are with me. You carry my griefs, because you grieve for my sake. You passed through the narrow doorway from death to life, to make it wide enough for all to follow. Nothing can ever now separate me from your love.

Bernard of Clairvaux

O Lord, holy father, show us what kind of man it is who is hanging for our sakes on the cross, whose suffering causes the rocks themselves to crack and crumble with compassion, whose death brings the dead back to life.

Let my heart crack and crumble at the sight of him. Let my soul break apart with compassion for his suffering. Let it be shattered with grief at my sins for which he dies. And finally let it be softened with devoted love for him.

Bonaventura

O God, we pray that the burden of sin which we carry on our souls may be dissolved for ever in the blood of our Lord Jesus Christ. And, free from this deadly weight, may our souls raise with him to eternal life.

The Gelasian Sacramentary

Good Jesu, my God and my all,
Be thou all to me,
Be thou all in me,
That I may be all thine,
And all thy will mine.

Make me cheerful under every cross,
For love of thy Cross;
Take from me all which displeases thee,
Or hinders thy love in me,
That I may deeply love thee.
Melt me with thy love,
That I may be all love,
And with my whole being love thee.

Good Jesu, who gavest thyself for me,
Give me of the fullness of thy love,
That for all thy love,
With thy love, I may love thee.

E.B. Pusey

EASTER

I see flames of orange, yellow and red
shooting upwards to the sky, piercing the
whole clouds.

I see the clouds themselves chasing the
flames upwards, and I feel the air itself
reaching for the heavens.

Down below I see great, grey rocks
beating against the earth, as if they were
pushing their way down to hell.

At your resurrection that which is light
and good rises up with you, and that which
is heavy and evil is pushed downwards.

At your resurrection goodness breaks free
from evil, life breaks free from death.

Adam of St Victor

O Lord God, our Father. You are the light
that can never be put out; and now you give
us a light that shall drive away all the
darkness. You are love without coldness,
and you have given us such warmth in our
hearts that we can love all when we meet.
You are the life that defies death, and you
have opened for us the way that leads to
eternal life.

None of us is a great Christian; we are all humble and ordinary. But your grace is enough for us. Arouse in us that small degree of joy and thankfulness of which we are capable, to the timid faith which we can muster, to the cautious obedience which we cannot refuse, and thus to the wholeness of life which you have prepared for all of us through the death and resurrection of your Son. Do not allow any of us to remain apathetic or indifferent to the wondrous glory of Easter, but let the light of our risen Lord reach every corner of our dull hearts.

Karl Barth

Lord, you have passed over into new life, and you now invite us to pass over also. In these past days we have grieved at your suffering and mourned at your death. We have given ourselves over to repentance and prayer, to abstinence and gravity. Now at Easter you tell us that we have died to sin. Yet, if this is true, how can we remain on earth? How can we pass over to your risen life, while we are still in this world. Will we not be just as meddlesome, just as lazy, just as selfish as before? Will we not still be bad-tempered and stubborn, enmeshed in all the vices of the past. We pray that as we pass over with you, our faces will never look back. Instead, let us, like you, make heaven on earth.

Bernard of Clairvaux

Rise, beloved Christ, like a dove rising high in the sky, its white feathers glistening in the sun. Let us see your purity of soul.

Like a sparrow keeping constant watch over its nest of little ones, watch over us day and night, guarding us against all physical and spiritual danger.

Like a turtledove hiding its offspring from all attackers, hide us from the attacks of the Devil.

Like a swallow, swooping down towards the earth, swoop down upon us and touch us with your life-giving Spirit.

Bonaventura

The moment we have longed for has come; the night of our desires is here. What greater occupation could there be than for us to

proclaim the power of your resurrection!
This was the night when you shattered the
gates of hell, and you took up the victory
banner of heaven. This was the night when
you set us among the stars.

When your mother Mary gave birth to
you, she was overwhelmed with joy at your
beauty. Now we are overwhelmed with joy
at your power. The blood which flowed
from your side has washed away our sins.
Your body rising from the tomb has
promised us eternal life. Eternal are the
blessings which in your love you have
poured upon us.

The Gelasian Sacramentary

You have protected us, Jesus, from endless
  disaster.
You spread your hands over us like wings.
You poured your blood over the earth,
Because you loved us.
The anger which we deserved you turned
  away from us
And restored us to friendship with God.

The heavens may have your spirit, paradise
  your soul,

But the earth has your blood.
We celebrate the coming of your Spirit
  always:
The Spirit leads the mystic dance throughout
  the year.
But Easter comes and goes.
Power came from heaven to raise you from
  death,
So that we and all creatures could see you.
All living things gather round you at Easter.
There is joy, honour, celebration, delight.

The darkness of death is driven away.
Life is restored everywhere.
The gates of heaven are thrown open.
In you, risen Jesus, God has shown us
  himself,
So we can rise to him as gods.
The gates of hell are shattered.
In you, risen Jesus, those already dead rise to
  life,
Affirming the good news of eternal life.
Now your promise has been fulfilled.
Now the earth is singing and dancing.
Easter is our marriage ceremony.
At Easter, dear Jesus, you make us your
  brides.

Sealing the union with your Spirit.
The great marriage hall is full of guests,
All dressed for the wedding.
No-one is rejected for want of a wedding-
dress.
We come to you as spiritual virgins,
Our lamps are fresh and bright, with ample
oil,
The light within our souls will never go out.
The fire of grace burns in us all.

We pray you, our sovereign Christ,
Stretch out your strong hands over your
whole church
And over all your faithful people.
Defend, protect, and preserve them,
Fight and do battle for them, subdue the
invisible powers that oppose them.
Raise now the sign of victory over us
And grant that we may sing the song of
triumph.
May you rule for ever and ever.

Hippolytus

ASCENSION

To complete your seamless robe, and so to complete our faith, you ascended through the air into the heavens, before the very eyes of the apostles. In this way you showed that you are Lord of all, and are the fulfilment of all creation. Thus from that moment every human and every living creature should bow at your name. And, in the eyes of faith, we can see that all creation proclaims your greatness.

Bernard of Clairvaux

Lord Jesus, I put my faith in you. I place my hope in you, and I love you with my whole mind and my whole strength. When you rise up to heaven, I long to be carried up to heaven, that my faith may be vindicated, and my love rewarded.

Lord Jesus, as you sit upon your throne in heaven, redeem those who are lost, sanctify those who are redeemed, and give joy to those who are sanctified.

Bonaventura

O God, we give thanks that your Son Jesus
Christ, who has shared our earthly life, has
now ascended to prepare our heavenly life.
Grant that, through coming to know him by
faith on earth, we may come to know him by
sight in heaven.

The Gelasian Sacramentary

Good Jesu, exalted above the highest
  heavens,
But dwelling with the lowly,
Make me as a little lowly child,
Suspecting nothing,
Fearing nothing,
Mistrusting nothing;
But trusting my whole self with thee.
I am not worthy to kiss the hem of thy
  garment,
But do thou take me up in thy arms and
  bless me.

E.B. Pusey

PENTECOST

Who is this who smothers me with the most fragrant perfume? Who is this who transforms my ugliness into perfect beauty? Who is this who gives me the sweetest wine to drink, and the finest food to eat?

It is you, Holy Spirit. You turn me into a bride fit for Jesus Christ. You give me wine and food fit for a wedding in Heaven.

My heart was weary, but now it is eager for love. My soul was sad, but now it is full of joy.

Jesus gave his life for me. Now you, Holy Spirit, give me to him.

Adam of St Victor

Lord Jesus, as God's Spirit came down and rested upon you, may the same Spirit rest upon us, bestowing his sevenfold gifts.

First, grant us the gift of understanding, by which your precepts may enlighten our minds.

Second, grant us counsel, by which we may follow in your footsteps on the path of righteousness.

Third, grant us courage, by which we may ward off the Enemy's attacks.

Fourth, grant us knowledge, by which we can distinguish good from evil.

Fifth, grant us piety, by which we may acquire compassionate hearts.

Sixth, grant us fear, by which we may draw back from evil and submit to what is good.

Seventh, grant us wisdom, that we may taste fully the life-giving sweetness of your love.

Bonaventura

We beseech you, O Lord, to ignite our souls with love, faith and hope by the fire of your Holy Spirit. And may the wind of your Spirit so inspire our minds, that we may proclaim your gospel to others in words which they can understand.

The Gelasian Sacramentary

Personal and corporate devotion

SELF-OFFERING

You are great, Lord, and greatly to be
praised. Great is your power, and of your
wisdom there is no end. And man, who is
part of what you have created, desires to
praise you. Yes, even though he carries his
mortality wherever he goes, as the proof of
his sin and testimony of your justice, man
desires to praise you. For you have stirred
up his heart so that he takes pleasure in
praising you. You have created us for
yourself, and our hearts are restless until
they rest in you.

Augustine of Hippo

O beloved Father, whom I adore, help me to
forget myself entirely that I may think only
of you, and so be peaceful as if I were
already in eternity. May nothing trouble my
peace or make me leave you, O unchanging
One, but may each minute carry me further
into the depths of your mystery. Make my
soul your heaven, your dwelling, and your
bed. May I never leave you there alone but
be wholly present, wholly faithful, wholly

vigilant, wholly adoring, and wholly surrendered to you.

O beloved Christ, crucified by love, I wish to be a bride for your heart. I wish to cover you with glory. I wish to love you, even to die for you. But I can feel my weakness, so I beg you to clothe me with yourself, to overwhelm me, to possess me, to substitute yourself for me that my life may be your life. May every action of mine be movements of your soul.

Come to me as adorer, as restorer, as saviour. Eternal Word, I want to spend every day listening to you, learning from you. Then every night I want to gaze on you and bask in your radiant light.

O Spirit of love, consuming fire, come upon me and re-create me as another incarnation of the eternal Word. Thus my humanity may be Christ's humanity, revealing to the world the mystery of the Father. And when you, Spirit, have transformed me into the human image of Christ, then his Father will have become my Father.

O Trinity, my all, you are the immensity in which I can lose myself, the almighty power to which I can surrender, the holy ground in which I can bury myself, the infinitely beautiful light which I can contemplate for all eternity.

Elizabeth of Catez

Lord, of my heart, give me vision to inspire me, that, working or resting, I may always think of you.

Lord of my heart, give me light to guide me, that, at home or abroad, I may always walk in your way.

Lord of my heart, give me wisdom to direct me, that thinking or acting, I may always discern right from wrong.

Lord of my heart, give me courage to strengthen me, that amongst friends or enemies, I may always proclaim your justice.

Lord of my heart, give me trust to console me, that, hungry or well-fed, I may always rely on your mercy.

Lord of my heart, save me from empty praise, that I may always boast of you.

Lord of my heart, save me from worldly wealth, that I may always look to the riches of heaven.

Lord of my heart, save me from military prowess, that I may always seek your protection.

Lord of my heart, save me from vain knowledge, that I may always study your word.

Lord of my heart, save me from unnatural pleasures, that I may always find joy in your wonderful creation.

Heart of my own heart, whatever may befall me, rule over my thoughts and feelings, my words and action.

Celtic Prayers

I beseech you, merciful God, to allow me to drink from the stream which flows from your fountain of life. May I taste the sweet beauty of its waters, which spring from the very depths of your truth. O Lord, you are that fountain from which I desire with all my heart to drink. Give me, Lord Jesus, this water, that it may quench the burning spiritual thirst within my soul, and purify me from all sin.

I know, King of glory, that I am asking from you a great gift. But you give to your

faithful people without counting the cost,
and you promise even greater things in the
future. Indeed, nothing is greater than
yourself, and you have given yourself to
mankind on the cross. Therefore, in praying
for the waters of life, I am praying that you,
the source of those waters, will give yourself
to me. You are my light my salvation, my
food, my drink, my God.

Columbanus

Grant me, gracious Lord, a pure intention of
my heart, and a steadfast regard to thy glory
in all my actions. Possess my mind
continually with thy presence, and ravish it
with thy love, that my only delight may be,
to be embraced in the arms of thy protection.

John Cosin

I am not now mine, but thine. Therefore
claim me as thy right, keep me as thy charge,
and love me as thy child. Fight for me when
I am assaulted, heal me when I am
wounded, and revive me when I am
destroyed.

John Cosin

Lord, let me be obedient without arguing,
humble without feigning, patient without
grudging, pure without corruption, merry
without lightness, sad without mistrust,
sober without dullness, true without
doubleness, fearing thee without
desperation, and trusting in thee without
presumption.

John Cosin

Lord, since you exist, we exist. Since you are
beautiful, we are beautiful. Since you are
good, we are good. By our existence we
honour you. By our beauty we glorify you.
By our goodness we love you.

Lord, through your power all things were
made. Through your wisdom all things are
governed. Through your grace, all things are
sustained. Give us power to serve you,
wisdom to discern your laws, and grace to
obey them at all times.

Edmund of Abingdon

O Lord, guide my thoughts and my words.
It is not that I lack subjects for meditation.
On the contrary, I am crushed with the

weight of them. How many are your mercies God – mercies yesterday and today, and at every moment of my life, from before my birth, from before time itself began! I am plunged deep in mercies; I drown in them; they cover me, wrapping me round on every side.

Lord Jesus, we should all sing of your mercies – we, who were all created for everlasting glory redeemed by your blood. But if we all have cause to sing your praises, how much more cause have I? From childhood I have been surrounded by so many graces. My saintly mother taught me to know you, to love you, and, as soon as I could speak, to pray to you.

Despite so many blessings I drifted away from you for many years. I withdrew further and further from you, and my life became a death in your eyes. I enjoyed numerous worldly pleasures, and thought I was alive. but beneath the surface there was deep sadness, disgust, boredom, restlessness. Whenever I was alone a great melancholy came over me.

Yet, how good you are to me. You slowly

and patiently destroyed my worldly attachment. You broke down everything that prevented me from living for you. You showed me the futility and falsehood of my life in the world. Then you planted in my heart a tender seedling of love, so gradually my heart turned back to you. You gave me a taste for prayer, a trust in your word, a desire to imitate you.

Now I am overwhelmed by your blessings. O beloved Bridegroom there is nothing that you have not done for me. Now tell me what you want of me, how you expect me to serve you. Create in my thoughts, words and actions that which will give true glory to you.

Charles de Foucauld

Lord, shall we delay any longer our offering to you of all that we have and all that we are? Shall we keep back any longer the complete gift of our free will, which we cling too so stubbornly? Shall we refuse to stretch out our will on the wood of your cross, to

transfix it with the thorns and lance that
pierced you? Let our will be swallowed up
in the fire of your perfect, loving will! Let
our will burn for all eternity as a sacrifice to
you.

Francis of Sales

Draw me completely into yourself,
So that I might completely melt in your love.

Lay upon me, stamp upon me,
So that my stubborn pride might be
  destroyed.

Embrace me, kiss me,
So that my spiritual ugliness may turn to
  beauty.

Lock me into your chamber
So that I might never stray from your
  presence.

Johann Freylinghausen

In my prayers, dear Jesus, I am with you
  wholly.
If I meditate on the cross, I suffer with you.
If I meditate on the resurrection, I rise with
  you.
So daily I die and rise.

If I walk with you along the hot dusty roads,
I become hot, sweaty, tired, as you surely
  did.
If I hear you preach, my ears tingle with
  excitement,
And my heart is pierced by the sharpness of
  your words.
If I watch you heal people, I can feel your
  touch,
So my own body trembles at your power.

Let me walk with you during every minute
  of my life,
Let me constantly be inspired by your
  words,
Let me daily be renewed by your power,
That I may die to sin and rise to perfect
  righteousness.

Gemma Galgani

Thou who art over us,
Thou who art one of us,
Thou who art also within us,
May all see thee – in me also.
May I prepare the way for thee,
May I thank thee for all that shall fall to my
    lot,
May I also not forget the needs of others,
Keep me in thy love
As thou wouldest that all should be kept in
    mine.
May everything in this my being be directed
    to thy glory
And may I never despair.
For I am under thy hand,
And in thee is all power and goodness.

Dag Hammarskjöld

Give me a pure heart – that I may see
    thee,
A humble heart – that I may hear thee,
A heart of love – that I may serve thee,
A heart of faith – that I may abide in thee.

Dag Hammarskjöld

Before thee, Father
  In righteousness and humility,
With thee, Brother,
  In faith and courage,
In thee, Spirit,
  In stillness.

Dag Hammarskjöld

O Jesus, in whom we all may be made
desirable! O Lord, redeemer and saviour,
prince of all holiness and peace! We have
sinned, we have done amiss, we have fallen,
we have gone astray, we are not worthy so
much as to gather up the crumbs under the
table of God! Enter thou, therefore, into our
souls. Possess our spirits with thy spirit, our
body with thy body, our blood with thy blood.
Feed us with thyself, who art perfect
righteousness. Lay hold of us by thy grace,
who art the truth and the life. Uplift us, mould
us, transform us by thy own power into
thyself, into the image of the holy and the
eternal. We will shrink from no suffering, we
will endure all, in the energy of thy broken
body and outpoured blood, if only we may be

drawn upward into the likeness of thyself, into
the joy of thy holiness! Fill us with sorrow, if so
only thou canst fill us with thyself: for only by
abiding in thee, only by eating thy flesh and
drinking thy blood, only by fastening on the
grace of thy perfect, holy, and sufficient
oblation, can we hope to pass from death into
life, and to be raised up at the last day from the
lowliness of the grave to the holiness of
heaven!

Henry Scott Holland

Take, Lord, and receive all my freedom, my
memory, my intelligence and my will – all
that I have and possess. You, Lord, have
given those things to me. I now give them
back to you, Lord. All belongs to you.
Dispose of these gifts according to your will.
I ask only for your love and your grace, for
they are enough for me.

Ignatius of Loyola

I have so little time, so little space.
Take from me, that I may give.
Open wide that wound to let your Spirit in.

I must watch, I must wait, I must need, I
  must beg.
You live in the darkness. So be it.
Ah, grant me but this: that I stand in want
Till that want is so wide that only you can
  fill it.
Keep me from safe, warm acquiescence.
  Give me urgency and the ranging spirit.
Take all, that I may be all for you, that all
  from me may mean all from you, all for
  you.
May you be my all, in all.
Only your strength, your vision, your
  command, your wilderness.
Mine to follow after.
I fear, even as I say it, but I confess
I hold
I affirm.

Philip Jebb

Lord God, my beloved, if you still remember
my sins, and so withhold the blessing for
which I yearn, I beg you either to punish me
as I deserve, or to have mercy on me. If you

are waiting for me to behave well and do good to others, then give me the strength and the will to act as you want.

Why are you waiting? Why do you delay in pouring out the love for which I yearn? How can I behave well and love others, if you do not strengthen and guide me? How can I be worthy of you, if you do not make me worthy? How can I rise up to you, if you do not raise me up?

Surely you will not take from me the grace which you gave me in your dear Son Jesus Christ?

Surely the love which he revealed to all mankind will be granted to me? Why are you waiting?

The earth and the heavens are mine! All the people in the world, righteous and sinful alike, are mine! The angels, the saints and the martyrs, are mine! All these are mine because I would offer them all to you, in exchange for your love.

I give you my life, my all! Why are you waiting to receive it?

John of the Cross

Hear me, O God!
   A broken heart
   Is my best part;
Use still thy rod,
   That I may prove
   Therein, thy Love.

If thou hadst not
   Been stern to me,
   But left me free,
I had forgot
   My self and thee.

For sin's so sweet
   As minds ill bent
   Rarely repent,
Until they meet
   Their punishment.

Who more can crave
   Than thou hast done,
   That gav'st a Son
To free a slave?
   First made of nought,
   With all since bought.

Sin, Death, and Hell
  His glorious Name
  Quite overcame,
Yet I rebel
  And slight the same.

But I'll come in
  Before my loss,
  Me farther toss,
As sure to win
  Under his Cross.
                    Ben Jonson

Wherever I am, whatever I do, thou, Lord,
seest me: O, keep me in thy fear all day long.
Lord, give me grace to keep always a
conscience void of offence towards thee and
towards men.

Lord, teach me so to number my days, that
I may apply my heart to wisdom. O, let my
mouth be filled with thy praise, that I may
sing of thy glory and honour all the day
long.

                    Thomas Ken

Light without equal, so pure;
Beauty without peer, so serene;
We desire to be reborn with you.
Power without limits, so strong;
Glory without end, so majestic;
We desire to be reborn with you.

In your kingdom every flower blossoms
   continuously;
Every tree is always newly in leaf;
We desire to be reborn with you.
Music of sublime charm plays everywhere;
Perfume of sweetest fragrance fills the
   nostrils;
We desire to be reborn with you.

Thought of you fills our minds;
Love of you fills our hearts;
We desire to be reborn with you.
Desire for you fills our bodies;
Knowledge of you fills our souls;
We desire to be reborn with you.

Mahayana Buddhism

Lord, love me passionately,
Love me often,
Love me long.
The more passionately you love me, the
  more beautiful I become.
The more often you love me, the purer I
  become.
The longer you love me, the holier I become.
                              Mechthild of Magdeburg

Lord, because I am the lowest of all
  creatures,
You have raised me high above them to
  yourself.
Lord, because I have no earthly treasures,
You have poured upon me heavenly
  treasure.
Lord, because I am dressed in the grey rags
  of sin,
You have clothed me in the pure white robe
  of virtue.
Lord, because I desire the merest hovel for
  my home,
You have welcomed me to your eternal
  palace.
                              Mechthild of Magdeburg

I cannot dance, O Lord, unless you lead me.
If it is your will, I can leap with joy.
But you must show me how to dance and
 sing
By dancing and singing yourself!
With you I will leap towards love,
And from love I will leap to truth,
And from truth I will leap to joy,
And then I shall leap beyond all human
 senses.
There I will remain
And dance for evermore.

Mechthild of Magdeburg

Almighty eternal Father,
thou dost marry justice and mercy in thyself,
 God and man in thy Son,
might and peace in thy Spirit.
O! marry in me
the fear of thee and the love of thee,
the knowledge, and the practice, of thy will,
a contrite and a thankful heart,
the present and the eternal all day long.
Thyself, Lord, be the consort of my soul,
wedding immortal grace to mortal birth,

wedding my happiness with thy glory,
wedding my weakness and thy strength,
thy desires and my obedience,
thy Cross and my crown.
O! clothe me with thy wedding
   garment –
he that is joined to the Lord
is one spirit with him.
My Lord and Master, hear me pledge my
   troth:
with my body I thee worship,
with mine understanding, with my heart,
with all my worldly goods,
with all thy heavenly gifts,
I thee worship, thee adore.
Those, Lord, whom thou hast joined
   together
let no man, nothing, put asunder.

Eric Milner-White

Lord, put courage into my heart, and take
away all that may hinder me serving you.
Free my tongue to proclaim your goodness,
that all may understand me. Give me friends
to advise and help me, that by working

together our efforts may bear abundant fruit.
And, above all, let me constantly remember
that my actions are worthless unless they are
guided by your hand.

Mohammed

Lord, in you we put our trust. To you we
turn in times of need. To you we shall go at
the moment of death. Do not allow us to be
deceived and misled by the designs of those
whose hearts are evil. Forgive us for the evil
in our own hearts. You alone are mighty;
you alone are wise.

Mohammed

Holy God, you have shown me light and life.
You are stronger than any natural power.
Accept the words from my heart
That struggle to reach you.
Accept the silent thoughts and feelings
That are offered to you.
Clear my mind of the clutter of useless facts.
Bend down to me, and lift me in your arms.
Make me holy as you are holy.
Give me a voice to sing of your love to others.

Prayers from Papyri

God of Abraham, God of Isaac, God of
  Jacob,' not of the philosophers and
  scholars.
Certainty. Certainty. Emotion. Joy. Peace.
God of Jesus Christ.
'My God and your God'.
Your God shall be my God.
Forgetting the world and all things, except
  only God.
He can be found only by the ways taught in
  the Gospel.
Greatness of the human soul.
Righteous Father, the world has not known
  you, but I have known you.
Joy, joy, joy, tears of joy.
I have cut myself off from him.
'They have forsaken me, the fountain of
  living water.'
'My God, will you forsake me?'
May I not be cut off from him forever!
'This is life eternal, that they know you, the
  only true God, and Jesus Christ, whom you
  have sent.'
Jesus Christ,
Jesus Christ.
I have cut myself off from him, shunned

him, decried him, crucified him.
Let me never be cut off from him!
We cling to him only by the ways taught in
the Gospel.
Sweet and total renunciation.
Total submission to Jesus Christ and to my
director,
Eternal joy in return for one day's trial on
earth.
'I will not forget your word.'

Blaise Pascal

Lord, I am your ship.
Fill me with the gifts of your Holy Spirit.
Without you I am empty of every blessing,
And full of every sin.

Lord, I am your ship.
Fill me with a cargo of good works.
Without you, I am empty of every joy,
And full of vain pleasures.

Lord, I am your ship.
Fill me with love for you.

John Sergieff

Take me captive, Lord, in the sweet captivity of your Holy Spirit. May I be a prisoner of your Spirit's impulses. Let the actions that I perform, the words that I speak, and my innermost thoughts and feelings, be under your Spirit's compulsions. I want only to see what your Spirit lets me see, and go where your spirit allows. I am a joyful, willing captive!

John Sergieff

Lord, teach me to be generous to others with a willing and joyful heart, knowing that through generous actions I gain infinitely more spiritually than I lose materially. Let me not be influenced by those who meet poverty with indifference, who blame the past for their own misfortunes. O Lord, such hard-hearted people are so common that I meet them every day. Yet in hearing their cold attitudes, may my own heart be kindled anew to serve those who are hungry, thirsty or naked. And show me how my efforts may best be directed, to give greatest help to those in need.

John Sergieff

This is my prayer to thee, my Lord – strike, strike at the root of penury in my heart. Give me the strength to make my love fruitful in service. Give me the strength never to disown the poor or bend my knees before insolent might. Give me the strength to raise my mind high above daily trifles. And give me the strength to surrender my strength to thy will with love.

Rabindranath Tagore

Lord, open our eyes,
That we may see you in our brothers and
 sisters.
Lord, open our ears,
That we may hear the cries of the hungry,
 the cold, the frightened, the oppressed.
Lord, open our hearts,
That we may love each other as you love us.
Renew in us your spirit
Lord, free us and make us one.

Mother Teresa

Take, O Lord, and receive
All my liberty, my memory,
my understanding and my will,
all that I have and possess.
You have given them to me;
To you, O Lord, I restore them.
All things are yours:
Dispose of them according to your will.
Give me your love and your grace,
For this is enough for me.

Mother Teresa

Here I am, Lord – body, heart and soul.
Grant that with your love,
I may be big enough to reach the world,
And small enough to be at one with you.

Mother Teresa

Lord, may my desires change to your
desires. Lord, if a desire is good and
profitable, give me grace to fulfill it to your
glory. But if it be hurtful and injurious to my
soul's health, then remove it from my mind.

Thomas à Kempis

Loving God, who sees in us nothing that you
have not given yourself, make my body
healthy and agile, my mind sharp and clear,
my heart joyful and contented, my soul
faithful and loving. And surround me with
the company of men and angels who share
my devotion to you. Above all let me live in
your presence, for with you all fear is
banished, and there is only harmony and
peace. Let every day combine the beauty of
spring, the brightness of summer, the
abundance of autumn, and the repose of
winter. And at the end of my life on earth,
grant that I may come to see and know you
in the fullness of your glory.

Thomas Aquinas

Lord Jesus, you are the source of all holiness
and beauty: and yet you are holier and more
beautiful than we could ever imagine. You are
the source of knowledge and skill: and yet your
knowledge of truth and your skill in creation
far exceeds our greatest visions. You are the
source of glory and honour, power and dignity,
joy and gladness, fame and praise; yet we have

only the dimmest understanding of these many blessings, which you bestow upon us with such generosity. Above all, you are the source of sweetness and consolation, which bring true joy amidst the greatest sorrows.

O Lord Jesus Christ, spouse of my soul, lover of purity, Lord of creation, give me wings that I may fly to you. Set me free from all sin, that I may taste your sweetness. Embrace every thought in my mind and feeling in my heart, turning me into your perfect bride.

Thomas à Kempis

Lord, when my eye confronts my heart, and I realise that you have filled my heart with your love, I am breathless with amazement. Once my heart was so small in its vision, so narrow in its compassion so weak in its zeal for truth. Then you chose to enter my heart, and now in my heart I can see you, I can love all your people, and I have courage to proclaim the truth of your gospel to anyone and everyone. Like wax before a fire, my heart has melted under the heat of your love.

Count von Zinzendorf

My dearest Saviour! We beg of you this same blessed look, this same irresistible look, which you always fix on the souls who like to look upon you, who like to receive you, who are ready to share your wounds, and who are even prepared to die for you. May all souls on earth, high and low, rich and poor, yearn for your look. And let us for our part testify amongst those we meet to your sacrificial love, that the number of those who succumb to your look may grow and grow. Indeed we promise that we shall not rest until we are able to look upon you, and say: 'Lord, we have filled every place in heaven, by bringing every soul on earth under the bright light of your love'.

Count von Zinzendorf

CONFESSION AND FORGIVENESS

Lord, why did you enlighten a soul so dark?
Why did you capture a soul that constantly
tries to flee from you? Why did you purify a
soul so foul?

I shudder when I think of the horrors that
were in store for me, if I had continued on
the path which I was treading. But even now
I feel that Hell is the only proper place for
me. O God, I want to hide from you, because
I feel too filthy and ugly to appear in your
presence.

Yet whenever I try to escape from you, I
find that you are still with me, because your
presence is everywhere. Weeping brings me
no peace of comfort, and repentance seems
to bring no sense of forgiveness. Dear God,
punish me as I deserve, so that I may be free
of this burden of sin.

Catherine of Genoa

Forgive me O Lord, O Lord forgive me my
sins, the sins of my youth, and my present
sins, the sin that my parents cast upon me,
original sin, and the sins that I cast upon my

children, in an ill example; actual sins, sins which are manifest to all the world, and sins which I have so laboured to hide from the world, as that now they are hid from mine own conscience, and mine own memory. Forgive me my crying sins, and my whispering sins, sins of uncharitable hate, and sins of unchaste love, sins against thee and against thy power O almighty Father, against thy wisdom, O glorious Son, against thy goodness, O blessed Spirit of God; and sins against him and him, against superiors and equals, and inferiors; and sins against me and me, against mine own soul, against my body, which I have loved better than my soul. Forgive me O Lord, in the merits of thy Christ and my Jesus, thine Anointed, and my Saviour. Forgive me my sins, all my sins, and I will put Christ to no more cost, nor thee to more trouble, for any reprobation or malediction that lay upon me, otherwise than as a sinner.

John Donne

O Lord Jesus, thou, whom we, by our sins, have robbed of that good gift of joy, which might have been thine! Thou, whom we have forbidden to partake of flesh and blood, except at bitter cost of that agony and blood-sweat! O holy, merciful, all-forgiving redeemer, teach us more worthy to repent of the terror and horror of our fall, by the memory of that innocent gladness with which we should have gone with thee to the altar of God, to offer there, no sorrow-stricken, death-stained, sin-worn sacrifice, but the unshrinking homage of a spotless heart!

Henry Scott Holland

Through your whole life, O Lord Jesus Christ, you suffered that I might be saved. And yet your suffering is not at an end. For still you have to bear with me, stumbling as I walk along the path, and constantly going astray. How often have I become impatient, wanting to give up your way! And how often have you given me the encouragement and helping hand that I need. Every day I increase the burden that you must bear; but just as I am impatient so you are infinitely patient.

Søren Kierkegaard

Your love covers the multitude of my sins. So when I am fully aware of my sin, when before the justice of heaven only wrath is pronounced upon me, then you are the only person to whom I can escape. If I try to cover myself against the guilt of sin and the wrath of heaven, I will be driven to madness and despair. But if I rely on you to cover my sins, I shall find peace and joy. You suffered and died on the cross to shelter us from our guilt, and take upon yourself the wrath that we deserve. Let me rest under you, and may you transform me into your likeness.

Søren Kierkegaard

Without you, I should founder helplessly in my own dull and groping narrowness. I could never feel the pain of longing, not even deliberately resign myself to being content with this world, had not my mind again and again soared over its own limitations into the hushed reaches which are filled by you alone, the Silent Infinite. Where should I flee before you, when all my yearning for the unbounded, even my bold trust in my littleness, is really a confession of you?

But when I love you, when I manage to break out of the narrow circle of self and leave behind the restless agony of unanswered questions, when my blinded eyes no longer look merely from afar and from the outside upon your unapproachable brightness, and much more when you yourself, O Incomprehensible One, have become through love the inmost centre of my life, then I can bury myself entirely in you, O mysterious God, and with myself all my questions.

Karl Rahner

Lord, enlighten us to see the beam that is in our own eye, and blind us to the mote that is in our brother's. Let us feel our offences with our hands, make them great and bright before us like the sun, make us eat them and drink them for our diet. Blind us to the offences of our beloved, cleanse them from our memories, take them out of our mouths for ever. Help us at the same time with the grace of courage, that we be none of us cast down when we sit lamenting amid the ruins of our happiness or our integrity. Touch us

with fire from the altar, that we may be up
and doing to rebuild our city.

Robert Louis Stevenson

Jesus, you have been very patient with me
until now, and it is true that I have never
strayed far from you. But I know, and you
know, how often in my wretched
imperfection I allow myself to be distracted,
when I should be looking steadily at the Sun
which claims all my attention. I am like a
bird, picking up a piece of grain first on this
side, then on that side, running off to catch a
worm, coming across a pond and wetting its
feathers there, and even having a look at
some pretty flowers it passes. Since I cannot
compete with the eagles, I am more ready to
occupy my mind with the trifles of earth.

But, dear Jesus, after all these infidelities, I
don't rush away into a corner and weep. I
turn back to the Sun which is the centre of
my love and dry my bedraggled wings in its
rays. I tell the Father all about my faults,
down to the last details. I throw myself
recklessly on Him, as the best way to regain

control of myself, and so win a greater measure of your love. After all, haven't you told us that you came to call sinners, not the righteous?

Thérèse of Lisieux

Shepherds search for their lost sheep, but for their own profit. Men seek their lost property, but out of self-interest. Travellers visit foreign countries, but for their own benefit. Kings offer ransoms for prisoners, but out of political calculation. But why have you searched for me? Why have you sought me out? Why have you visited this hostile earth where I live? Why have you ransomed me with your blood? I am not worthy of such effort. Indeed in my sin I have wilfully tried to escape from you so you would not find me. I have wanted to become a god myself, deciding for myself what is good and bad according to my own whims and lusts. I have provoked you and insulted you. Why do you bother with me?

Tychon of Zadonsk

I stand before you – I for whose sake you came to earth. Look upon me, and you will see nothing but my need for salvation. Look upon me, and you may choose to condemn me to everlasting hell. Indeed, I would have no grounds for complaint if you send me to hell, because it is what I deserve. Yet if that was your intention, you would not have come. Your presence tells me that you are merciful, that you are ready to forgive me, that you want to save me from hell and prepare me for heaven. You love me, though I have given you no cause to love. You love me, though so often I have hated you. I stand before you now, to beg your mercy. Grant that, as you look upon me, I may look upon you with the eyes of faith, gazing upon your infinite beauty.

Tychon of Zadonsk

INTERCESSIONS

O God of truth, the Prince of peace, let there be peace and truth in our days; let all that believe be of one heart and of one soul.

O Thou who breakest not the bruised reed, who quenchest not the smoking flax, establish all them that stand in truth and grace, restore them that are falling through error or sin.

I beseech thee, Lord, of thy mercy, let thine anger be turned away from this city and from this house; for we have sinned against thee. Be thou pleased favourably to regard this place and all this land, tempering justice with mercy.

Grant that I may love them that love me, even though unknown to me; and bring them, as me, into thy heavenly kingdom, and grant that I may show them the mercy of God, by remembering them in my prayers; that I, with those for whom I have prayed, and those for whom I am in any way bound to pray, and with all the people of God, may have an entrance into thy kingdom, there to appear in righteousness and be satisfied with glory.

Lancelot Andrewes

O God, our Father, there are no two of us here with the same need. You know our needs. Bless us as each one of us needs. Specially bless those who are in the middle of some specially difficult time:
Those who have some specially difficult task to face or some specially difficult examination to sit;
Those who have some specially difficult problem to solve;
Those who have some specially difficult decision to take;
Those who have some specially difficult temptation to resist;
Those who have some specially difficult doubt through which to think their way.

Speak to those who are
    Evading some decision;
    Shrinking some task;
    Putting off some duty;
    Playing with fire;
    Wasting their time;

Throwing away their opportunities.
Tell them that they dare not bring shame to
themselves and disappointment to those
who love them.

Speak to those who are successful, that
they may be kept from all pride and self-
conceit; speak to those who are too self-
confident, that they may not be riding for a
fall; speak to those who are too sure that
they are right and too sure that everyone
else is wrong, that they may be kept from
intolerance. Help those who are shy.
Remember those who are in disgrace and in
prison, and keep them from despair.

William Barclay

Lord, bless the world, and specially these
kingdoms, with wise godly, just and
peaceable princes and inferior judges and
magistrates and guide, protect and perfect
them for the common good and the
promoting of godliness and suppressing of
sin. And bless all churches with able, godly,
faithful pastors, that are zealous lovers of
God and goodness and the people's souls.
And save the nations and churches from

oppressing tyrants and deceivers, and from
malignant enemies to serious piety. And
cause subjects to live in just obedience and in
love and peace. Bless families with wise,
religious governors, who will carefully
instruct their children and servants and
restrain them from sin and keep them from
temptation. Teach children and servants to
fear God and honour and obey their
governors.

Richard Baxter

Be kind to your little children, Lord. Be a
gentle teacher, patient with our weakness
and stupidity. And give us the strength and
discernment to do what you tell us, and so
grow in your likeness.

May we all live in the peace that comes
from you. May we journey towards your
city, sailing through the waters of sin
untouched by the waves, borne serenely
along by the Holy Spirit. Night and day may
we give you praise and thanks, because you
have shown us that all things belong to you.
To you, the essence of wisdom, the
foundation of truth, be glory for evermore.

Clement of Alexandria

We pray to you, Lord, with honest hearts, in tune with one another, entreating you with sighs and tears, as befits our humble position – placed, as we are, between the spiritually weak who have no concern for you, and the saints who stand firm and upright before you.

We pray that you may soon come to us, leading us from darkness to light, oppression to freedom, misery to joy, conflict to peace. May you drive away the storms and tempest of our lives, and gentle calm.

We pray that you will care for us, as a father cares for his children.

Cyprian of Carthage

When, good Lord, will you manifest yourself to us in bright sunshine? Yes, we are slow to understand and slow to see. But we are quick to believe; and we believe that if you chose to reveal yourself to us, you could do so this very day.

Dear Lord, please appear to us, at dawn or at dusk or at the height of day. Come to our table at mealtimes, that we may share our meals with you. Come to our bed, that we

may share our rest with you. Come to us at
our prayers, that we may rejoice and be glad.
Gilbert of Hoyland

Move our hearts with the calm, smooth flow
of your grace. Let the river of your love run
through our souls. May my soul be carried
by the current of your love, towards the
wide, infinite ocean of heaven.

Stretch out my heart with your strength, as
you stretch out the sky above the earth.
Smooth out any wrinkles of hatred or
resentment. Enlarge my soul that I may
know more fully your truth.
Gilbert of Hoyland

Gracious Father, we humbly beseech thee for
thy universal church. Fill it with all truth, in
all truth with all peace. Where it is corrupt,
purge it; and where it is in error, direct it;
where it is superstitious, rectify it where
anything is amiss, reform it; where it is right,
strengthen and confirm it; where it is in
want, furnish it; where it is divided and rent
asunder, make up the breaches thereof, O
thou holy one of Israel.
William Laud

Lord, bless this kingdom, we beseech thee:
may religion and virtue increase amongst us,
that there may be peace within the gates,
and plenty within the palaces of it. In peace,
we beseech thee, so preserve it, that it
corrupt not; in war so defend it, that it suffer
not; in plenty, so order it, that it riot not; in
want, so pacify and moderate it, that it may
patiently and peaceably seek thee, the only
full supply both of men and state; that so it
may continue a place and a people to do
thee service to the end of time.

William Laud

Replenish our actions with amiableness and
beauty, that they may be answerable to
thine, and like unto thine in sweetness and
value. That as thou in all thy works art
pleasing to us, we in all our works may be so
to thee; our own actions as they are pleasing
to thee being an offspring of pleasures
sweeter than all.

Thomas Traherne

Supreme One, you are an obscure mystery to us. You made all things and can purify all things. You are far beyond our understanding. Even to speak to you is to enter an unknown region. Yet your light shines on all creatures, and your wonder illumines their souls. We beg you to leave your bright celestial palace in heaven, and come to this dusty world. Reveal yourself to us. Use your power to extinguish all evil and banish all sickness. Give peace to troubled souls. Reconcile those who are enemies, turning them into friends. Show us how we should live, that we may learn to obey you in all things.

Mahayana Buddhism

Why do you stand far off, O Lord? Why do you hide yourself in times of trouble? In their arrogance the wicked exploit the poor, catching them in schemes which they have devised. These wicked men are proud of their evil desires, and those who are greedy curse and reject you. So the helpless victims, lie crushed, while those who have defeated them by their brute strength say to themselves: 'God does not care; he has closed his eyes and will never see me.'

O Lord, punish those wicked men, and give help to their victims. How can you allow the wicked men to despise you, saying 'God will not call me to account.' You do see what is happening. You do take notice of trouble and suffering, and are always ready to help. Those who are weak put their trust in you, because in times past you have protected them.

You will listen, O Lord, to the prayers of the lowly, and give them courage. You will hear the cries of the oppressed and the orphaned, and give them justice.

Book of Psalms

We thank thee, Lord, for the glory of the late days and the excellent face of thy sun. We thank thee for good news received. We thank thee for the pleasures we have enjoyed and for those we have been able to confer. And now, when the clouds gather and the rain impends over the forest and our house, permit us not to be cast down. Let us not lose the savour of past mercies and past pleasures; but, like the voice of a bird singing in the rain, let grateful memory survive in the hour of darkness. If there be in front of us any painful duty, strengthen us with the grace of courage; if any act of mercy, teach us tenderness and patience.

Robert Louis Stevenson

THANKSGIVING

You are holy, Lord, the only God, and your
    deeds are wonderful.
You are strong.
    You are great.
    You are Most High,
    You are almighty.
    You, holy Father, are
    King of heaven and earth.
You are Three and One,
    Lord God, all good.
    You are Good, all Good, supreme Good,
    Lord God, living and true.
You are love,
    You are wisdom.
    You are humility,
    You are endurance.
    You are rest,
    You are peace.
    You are joy and gladness.
    You are justice and moderation.
    You are all our riches,
    And you suffice for us.
You are beauty.
    You are gentleness.

You are our protector,
You are our guardian and defender.
You are our courage.
You are our haven and our hope.
You are our faith,
    Our great consolation.
    You are our eternal life,
    Great and wonderful Lord,
    God almighty,
    Merciful Saviour.

St Francis of Assisi

Blessed art thou, O Lord, who has created
and brought me forth into this life, and hast
ordered that I should be a living soul and
not senseless matter; a man, not a brute;
civilised, not savage; free, not a slave;
legitimate, not spurious; of good parentage,
not of vile extraction and as vile myself;
endued with sense, not an idiot; sound in
sense, not blind nor deaf; sound in limbs, not
halt nor maimed; educated, not neglected; a
Christian, not a pagan; preserved from
dangers and infamy, not overwhelmed
thereby in the days of peace, not tossed in
tempestuous struggles; of competent

fortune, so that I need neither to flatter nor to borrow; set free from many sins; endued with the gifts of grace, in redemption and calling; with the gifts of nature and fortune, who according to thine abundant mercy hath begotten us again into a lively hope by the resurrection of Jesus Christ from the dead, to an inheritance incorruptible and undefiled, and that fadeth not away, reserved in heaven for us; who hast blessed me with all spiritual blessings in heavenly things in Christ; who comfortest me in all my tribulation, that, as the sufferings of Christ abound in me, so my consolation also aboundeth by Christ. To thee, O God of my fathers, I give thanks; thee I praise, who hast in some measure endued me with wisdom and might, and hast made known unto me that which I desired of thee, and hast made known to me the king's matter; who hast made me the work of thine hands, the price of thy blood, the image of thy countenance, the servant of thy purchase, the seal of thy name, the child of thy adoption, a temple of thy spirit, a member of thy Church.

Lancelot Andrewes

My God and my All! What greater blessing can I receive than your love? What greater wealth can I possess than your grace? What greater pleasure can I enjoy than your presence? What greater sweetness can I taste than your body and blood? What greater wisdom can I know than your Gospel?

Your wisdom is so simple that even fools like myself can understand it. Your holy communion is so generously given that even sinners like me are allowed to receive it. Your presence is everywhere so that even someone with such a dull mind as I have can find you. Your grace is such a constant source of reassurance that I can trust you completely for all my spiritual and material needs. And your love is so warm and so forgiving that even a cold, hard heart like my own is melted.

Thomas à Kempis

O adorable Trinity! What hast thou done for me? Thou hast made me the end of all things, and all the end of me. I in all, and all in me. In every soul whom thou hast created, thou hast given me the similitude of thyself to enjoy! Could my desires have aspired unto such treasures? Could my wisdom have devised such sublime enjoyment? O! thou hast done more for us than we could ask or think. I praise and admire, and rejoice in thee: who are infinitely infinite in all thy doings.

Thomas Traherne

O adorable and eternal God! Hast thou made me a free agent? And enabled me if I please to offend thee infinitely? What other end couldst thou intend by this, but that I might please thee infinitely? That having the power of pleasing or displeasing, I might be the friend of God? Of all exaltations in all worlds this is the greatest. To make a world for me was much, to command angels and men to love me was much, to prepare eternal joys for me was more. But to give me a power of pleasing or displeasing, might please thee and myself infinitely, in being pleasing!

Thomas Traherne

How shall I repay your generosity, O my Lover? How shall I repay you for all you have given me? If I had died a thousand times for your sake, it would be as nothing. You are my Lord, and I am just clay and ashes, a worthless sinner, who deserves to die thousands upon thousands of deaths. How shall I thank you, who suffered dishonour, insult, mockery, scourging, and death for my sake? How shall I, who has nothing, reward you who gave everything? I have ruined my own soul, which was given by you. And now the only merit my soul possesses is that which you have bestowed, in your forgiving love. The only thing I can return to you is my prayer, that time I devote each day speaking and listening to you. Receive my prayer, as a tiny token of my enormous gratitude.

Tychon of Zadonsk

COMMUNION

Lord, I acknowledge that I am far from
  worthy
To approach and touch this sacrament.
But I trust in that mercy
Which caused you to lay down your life for
  sinners,
That they might be saved from sin.
So I, a sinner, presume to receive these gifts.
Make me, O Lord, so to perceive with lips
  and heart
And know by faith and by love,
That by virtue of this sacrament
I may die to sin as you died,
And rise to fullness of life as you rose.
May I be made worthy
To become a member of your holy body,
A stone in your living temple
And let me rejoice forever
In your eternal love.

Anselm of Canterbury

You, Lord, are the bread of life and the well
of holiness. Just as you feed me day by day
with the food that sustains my body,

keeping me alive on earth, I pray that you
will feed my soul with the spiritual bread of
eternity, making me ready for heaven. Just
as you satisfy my bodily thirst with cool
water from the rivers and streams, I pray
that you will pour the water of holiness into
my soul, making my every word and action
a joyful sign of your love.

Basil of Caesarea

We do not presume to come to this thy table,
O merciful Lord, trusting in our own
righteousness, but in thy manifold and great
mercies. We are not worthy so much as to
gather up the crumbs under thy table, but
thou art the same Lord whose property is
always to have mercy. Grant us therefore,
gracious Lord, so to eat the flesh of thy dear
Son Jesus Christ, and to drink his blood that
our sinful bodies may be made clean by his
body, and our souls washed through his
most precious blood, and that we may
evermore dwell in him, and he in us.

The Book of Common Prayer

We give you thanks, Father,
for the holy vine of your servant, David,
which you have made known to us
through Jesus, your child.

Glory to you throughout the ages.

We give you thanks, Father,
for the life and knowledge you have sent us,
through Jesus, your child.

Glory to you throughout the ages.

As the ingredients of this bread,
once scattered over the mountains,
were gathered together and made one,
so may your church gather people
from the ends of the earth,
to become one in your kingdom.

The Didache

We give you thanks, holy Father,
for your holy name,
which you planted in our hearts;
and for the knowledge, faith and
  immortality

which you sent us through Jesus Christ, your
  child.

Glory to you throughout the ages.

You created everything, sovereign Lord,
for the glory of your name.
You gave food and drink to men
for their enjoyment,
and as a cause for thanksgiving.
And to us you have given
spiritual food and spiritual drink,
bestowing on us the promise of eternal life.
Above all we thank you
for the power of your love.

Glory to you throughout the ages.

Deliver your church, Lord, from all evil
and teach it to love you perfectly.
You have made it holy.
Build it up from the four winds
And gather it into the kingdom
for which you have destined it.
Power and glory to you throughout the ages.
                                        The Didache

Almighty God, Father of our Lord Jesus
Christ, we beg you that when we receive this
sacred mystery it may bring us blessing.
May Christ's body and blood not bring
condemnation upon us, but rather ennoble
all who receive it.

Eternal God, to whom that which is
invisible is as clear as that which is visible:
before you your people bow their heads,
submitting to you their hard hearts and
unruly bodies. Send down blessings from
your glorious dwelling on these men and
women, lending to their prayers a ready ear.
Hold them upright with your strong hand,
controlling all their evil passions. Preserve
their bodies and souls, filling them with faith
in your gospel and awe at your majesty.

Hippolytus

Lord, make my eyes walls of tears, that
when I receive your body tears of devotion
may pour down my cheeks. You are my joy,
Lord my bliss and my comfort. You are all
the treasure I have in this world. I want no
earthly pleasure; I want only you. And so,
dearest Lord, let your body which I now

receive be your pledge that you will never
forsake me, for all eternity.

Margery Kempe

Just as a grain of wheat must die in the earth
in order to bring forth a rich harvest, so your
Son died on the cross to bring a rich harvest
of love. Just as the harvest of wheat must be
ground into flour to make bread, so the
suffering of your Son brings us the bread of
life. Just as bread gives our bodies strength
for our daily work, so the risen body of your
Son gives us strength to obey your laws.

Thomas Münzer

All-powerful, everlasting God, I came to you
as a man sick, in need of life-giving
medicine; as useless, to bathe under your
fountain of mercy; as blind, seeking your
eternal light; as a beggar, pleading for your
spiritual treasure. I implore you in your
abundant kindness to cure my sickness,
cleanse my impurity, enlighten my
blindness, and enrich my poverty. May this
bread and wine be not only signs of such

grace, but also the true source of grace. In receiving the body of your Son, let me become a member of your mystical body. And grant that, while on earth I must see him under the veil of food and drink, in heaven I may behold him face to face.

Thomas Aquinas

When I approached the altar to receive you in the blessed sacrament, my hair stood on end. Then my legs went weak, and I felt as if I were about to collapse under the weight of your majesty. In the tiny piece of bread you revealed to me you grandeur and your purity. Since I am so wretched and so filthy, I should have felt terrified of your presence. But instead I felt comforted and reassured in the knowledge that you, the King of kings, were about to give yourself in love to me.

Teresa of Avila

God's care

CREATION

O Son of God, perform a miracle for me:
change my heart.
You, whose crimson blood redeems
mankind, whiten my heart.
It is you who makes the sun bright and the
ice sparkle; you who makes the rivers flow
and the salmon leap.
Your skilled hand makes the nut tree
blossom, and the corn turn golden; your
spirit composes the songs of the birds and
the buzz of the bees.
Your creation is a million wondrous
miracles, beautiful to behold. I ask of you
just one more miracle: beautify my soul.

Celtic Prayers

Most high, omnipotent, righteous Lord, to
you be all praise, glory, honour and blessing.
To you alone are they due, and no man is
worthy to mention you.

Praise be to you, my Lord, for all your
creatures, above all Brother Sun, who gives
us the light of day. He is beautiful and
radiant with great splendour, and so is like

you most high Lord.

Praise be to you, my Lord, for Sister Moon and the stars. In heaven you fashioned them, clear and precious and beautiful.

Praise be to you, my Lord, for Brother Wind, and for every kind of weather, cloudy or fair, stormy or serene, by which you cherish all that you have made.

Praise be to you, my Lord, for Sister Water, which is useful and humble and precious and pure.

Praise be to you, my Lord, for Brother Fire, by whom you lighten the night, for he is beautiful and playful and robust and strong.

Praise be to you, my Lord, for those who forgive sins in your love, and for those who bear sickness and tribulation.

Blessed are those who endure in peace, for by you, most high Lord, they shall be crowned.

Praise be to you, my Lord, for our Sister Bodily Death, from whom no living person can escape. Pity those who die in mortal sin.

Blessed are those who in death are found obedient to your most holy will, for death shall do them no harm.

Praise and bless my Lord, giving him
thanks and serving him with great humility.
St Francis of Assisi

O my great and good Creator, how much I
owe to you, that in your mercy you raised
me from nothing to make me what I am.
What can I possibly do to bless your name or
thank you enough for your inestimable
goodness?

Yet, my Creator, instead of uniting myself
to you by loving service, my inordinate
desires have made me a rebel. I have cut
myself off from you by preferring sin,
dishonouring you as if you were not my
Creator.

O my God, with all my heart I offer you
myself, as you have made me. I dedicate and
consecrate myself to you.
Francis of Sales

We come into thy house, our home
once more to give thanks:
for earth and sea and sky in harmony of
colour,

the air of the eternal seeping through the
  physical,
the everlasting glory dipping into time.
We praise thee.

For nature resplendent:
growing beasts, mergent crops, singing
  birds,
and all the gayness of the green.
We bless thee.

For swift running tides, resistant waves, thy
  spirit on the waters,
the spirit of the inerrant will,
Striving with the currents that are also thine.
We bless thee.
O Lord: how marvellous are thy works.
In majesty hast thou created them.

George Macleod

God, you are everywhere
present invisible
near to us speaking –
the silence awaits you
mankind exists for you
men see and know you.

Men made of flesh and bone
men of light and of stone
men of hard stone and blood
a flow unstaunchable
mankind your people
your city on earth.

Earth is all that we are
dust is all that we make,
breathe into us, open us,
make us your earth
your heaven new made
your peace upon earth.

Huub Oosterhuis

O Lord my God, how great you are! You are
clothed with honour and majesty; you cover
yourself with light. You stretch out the
heavens like a tent, and build your home on
the waters above. You make the clouds your
chariots, and you ride on the wings of the
wind. The winds are your messengers, and
flashes of lightning your servants.

Yet set the earth firmly on its foundations,
so that it could never be moved. You placed
the oceans over it like a robe, and the waters

covered the mountains. At your rebuke the
waters fled, flowing over the mountains and
into the valleys to the place you have made
for them. You marked a boundary which
they should not pass, to keep them from
covering the earth again.

You make springs gush forth in the
valleys, and rivers run between the hills.
They provide water for wild animals to
drink. In the trees near by the birds make
their nests and sing. From the sky you send
rain on the hills, and the earth is filled with
your blessings. You make the grass grow for
the cattle, and plants for men to cultivate, so
that he can bring food from the earth, wine
to gladden his heart, olive-oil to make his
face shine, and bread to give him strength.

You created the moon to mark the months;
the sun knows the time for setting. You made
the night when all the beauty of the forest
creep out. The young lions roar while they
hunt, looking for the food, which God
provides. When the sun rises they go back
and lie down in their den. Then the people go
out to work, labouring until evening.

Lord, you have made so many things,

fashioning them with such wisdom. The earth is filled with your creatures, and the oceans teem with countless fish.

All depend on you to give them food when they need it. You give it to them, and they eat it; you provide food, and they are satisfied. When you turn away they are afraid. When you take away their breath they die, and go back to the dust from which they came. But when you give them breath, they are created, and you renew the face of the earth.

The Book of Psalms

God of creation and Lord of the sabbath: you created the heavens and the earth and rested on the seventh day. You commanded your ancient people to cease from their work and rest in your love. Save us from our frenetic religious activities and enable us to let go our neurotic anxieties. Reveal to us your glory that we may gaze upon your beauty and be filled with your love.

Brother Ramon

Lord Jesus, you who are as gentle as the
human heart, as fiery as the forces of nature, as
intimate as life itself, you in whom I can melt
away and with whom I must have mastery
and freedom: I love you as a world, as this
world which has captivated my heart; and it is
you, I now realize, that my brother-men those
who do not believe, sense and seek throughout
the magic immensities of the cosmos.

Lord Jesus, you are the centre towards
which all things are moving: if it be possible,
make a place for us all in the company of
those elect and holy ones whom your loving
care has liberated one by one from the chaos
of our present existence and who now are
being slowly incorporated into you in the
unity of the new earth.

Teilhard de Chardin

What, O my Lord, could I desire to be which
thou hast not made me! If thou hast
expressed thy love in furnishing the house,
how gloriously doth it shine in the possessor!
My limbs and members when rightly prized,
are comparable to the fine gold, but that they
exceed it. The topaz of Ethiopia and the gold

of Ophir are not to be compared to them. What diamonds are equal to my eyes; what labyrinths to my ears; what gates of ivory, or ruby leaves to the double portal of my lips and teeth? Is not sight a jewel? Is not hearing a treasure? Is not speech a glory? O my Lord, pardon my ingratitude, and pity my dullness who am not sensible of these gifts. The freedom of thy bounty hath deceived me. These things were too near to be considered. Thou presentedst me with thy blessings, and I was not aware. But now I give thanks and adore and praise thee for thine inestimable favours.

Thomas Traherne

Homage to you, Breath of Life, for the whole universe obeys you. You are the ruler of all things on earth, and the foundation of the earth itself.

Homage to you, Breath of Life, in the crashes of thunder and in the flashes of lightning. The rain you send gives food to the plants and drink to the animals.

Homage to you, Breath of Life, in the changing seasons, in the hot dry sunshine and the cold rain. There is comfort and beauty in every kind of weather.

The plants themselves rejoice in your bounty, praising you in the sweet smell of their blossom. The cattle rejoice, praising you in the pure white milk they give.

Homage to you, Breath of Life, in our breathing out and breathing in. At every moment, whatever we are doing, we owe you praise and thanksgiving.

Homage to you, Breath of Life, in our birth and in our death. In the whole cycle of life you sustain and inspire us.

Homage to you, Breath of lIfe, in the love and friendship we enjoy. When we love one another, we reflect your infinite love.

Men and women rejoice in your bounty, praising you in poem and song. The little children rejoice, praising you in their innocent shrieks of laughter.

Atharva Veda

TRUTH AND FAITH

Supreme God, your light is brighter than the sun, your purity whiter than mountain snow, you are present wherever I go.

All people of wisdom praise you. So I too put faith in all your words, knowing that everything you teach is true. Neither the angels in heaven nor the demons in hell can know the perfection of your wisdom, for it is beyond all understanding.

Only your Spirit knows you; only you can know your true self. You are the source of all being, the power of all power, the ruler of all creatures. So you alone understand what you are.

In your mercy reveal to me all that I need to know, in order to find peace and joy. Tell me the truths that are necessary for the world in which I live.

Show me how I can meditate upon you, learning from you the wisdom that I need. I am never tired of hearing you, because your words bring life.

Arjuna

Almighty God, which dost make the minds
of all faithful men to be of one will: grant
unto thy people, that they may love the
thing, which thou commandest, and desire
that which thou dost promise, that among
the sundry and manifold changes of the
world, our heart may surely there be fixed,
where true joys are to be found.

Book of Common Prayer

I beg you, most loving Saviour, to reveal
yourself to us, that knowing you we may
desire you, that desiring you we may love
you, that loving you we may ever hold you
in our thoughts.

Columbanus

In holy things may be unholy greed.
Thou giv'st a glimpse of many a lovely thing
Not to be stored for use in any mind,
But only for the present spiritual need.
The holiest bread, if hoarded, soon will breed
The mammon-moth, the having pride.

George MacDonald

O, let me not always be thus dull and brutish; let not these scales of earthly affection always dim and blind mine eyes. O, thou that layedst clay upon the blind man's eyes, take away this clay from mine eyes, wherewith (alas) they are so daubed up that they cannot see heaven. Illuminate them from above, and in thy light let me see light. O, thou that has prepared a place for my soul, prepare my soul for that place; prepare it with holiness, prepare it with desire. And even while it sojourneth on earth, let it dwell in heaven with thee, beholding ever the beauty of thy face, the glory of thy saints and of itself.

Joseph Hall

I beg you, O God, to reveal to me the mystery of your love. Let your love be to me a new dawn at the end of a long night of gloom. Let your love be to me a new plan, showing the way of spiritual slavery. And let that plan be so simple that I can understand and follow it. Your love is like a white dove with orange flames bursting from its wings. The dove brings the promise of peace to my troubled soul, and the flames promise joy to my miserable heart.

Hildegard of Bingen

Dear Lord, give me the truths which are veiled by the doctrines and articles of faith, which are masked by the pious words of sermons and books. Let my eyes penetrate the veil, and tear off the mask, that I can see your truth face to face.

John of the Cross

O Lord Jesus Christ, I long to live in your presence, to see your human form and to watch you walking on earth. I do not want to see you through the darkened glass of tradition, nor through the eyes of today's values and prejudices. I want to see you as you were, as you are, and as you always will be. I want to see you as an offence to human pride, as a man of humility, walking amongst the lowliest of men, and yet as the saviour and redeemer of the human race.

Søren Kierkegaard

O Lord, the fulfilment of them that love thee, and the light that shineth upon them unto perfect day, who givest rest and refreshment to them that fall asleep in thee: grant unto us in all time of our service here on earth such a vision of thyself as shall guide us through the world's confusions, and support us in our conflicts and temptations.

Frederick Macnutt

O God, we are one with you. You have made us one with you. You have taught us that if we are open to one another, you dwell in us. Help us to preserve this openness and to fight for it with all our hearts. Help us to realize that there can be no understanding where there is mutual rejection. O God, in accepting one another wholeheartedly, fully, completely, we accept you, and we thank you, and we adore you, and we love you with our whole being, because our being is in your being, our spirit is rooted in your spirit. Fill us then with love, and let us be bound together with love as we go our diverse ways, united in this one spirit which makes you present in the world, and which

makes you witness to the ultimate reality
that is love. Love has overcome. Love is
victorious.

Thomas Merton

O Lord we know that if we put faith in our
own powers, we are building our lives on a
foundation of sand, and we shall be blown
over by the words of evil passion. May we
put our faith in you and you alone, building
our lives on the rock of your gospel, that we
may withstand even the fiercest gales of
temptation.

Mozarabic Sacramentary

Countless are your names, countless your
  dwelling-places;
The breadth of your kingdom is beyond our
  imagination.
Even to try and imagine your kingdom is
  foolish.
Yet through words and through music
We speak your name and sing your praise.
Words are the only tools we have to
  proclaim your greatness,
And music our only means of echoing your
  virtue.

You put words in our hearts and minds.
With words we can describe the glory of
   your creation,
And so our words can reflect your glory.
You put music in our hearts and minds.
With music we can echo the beauty of heaven,
And in our music we can express our
   deepest wish.
How can someone as insignificant as me
Express the vastness and wonder of your
   creation?
How can someone as sinful as me
Dare to hope for a place in heaven?
My only answer lies in the words and the
   music
Which you yourself have given me.

Nanak

Lord, put your hands on our eyes, that we
shall be able to see not only that which is
visible, but also that which is invisible. Let
our eyes be focused not only on that which is
present, but also that which is to come.
Unseal the heart's vision, that we may gaze
on God in his glory.

Origen

Lord, make me willing to be used by you.
May my knowledge of my unworthiness
never make me resist being used by you. May
the need of others always be remembered by
me, so that I may ever be willing to be used by
you.

And open my eyes and my heart that I may
this coming day be able to do some work of
peace for you.

Alan Paton

Heavenly Father: you have set sun, moon and
stars in their places and the music of the
spheres sings your praise; as I reflect upon
their glory and your handiwork, grant me a
greater awareness of the wonder of your
being and a deeper appreciation of your
tender love.

Brother Ramon

Lord, grant us eyes to see
Within the seed a tree,
Within the glowing egg a bird,
Within the shroud a butterfly:
Till taught by such, we see
Beyond all creatures thee,

And harken for thy tender word
And hear it, 'Fear not: it is I.'

Christina Rossetti

You possess me, Lord, and I possess you.
You have put your faith and hope in me.
and I have put my faith and hope in you.
My life, my honour, my happiness, my
  peace
All rest on you.
You can see me every second of my life;
Let me see you.
I pray that you will grant me a single
  moment
When I can look you face to face.
Then I will be able to give you
All my heart, all my love.
Do not wait until I have died,
But let me see you even here on earth.
I know I have no right to ask this favour
Because my heart is so luke-warm, so
  indifferent.
Make me worthy of such a privilege;
Make my heart ready to receive you.
And my soul ready to see you.

Simeon the Theodidact

You are like a tiger, compelling in your beauty, yet terrifying in your strength.

You are like a honey-comb on the branch of a tree; I can see the sweet honey, but the branch is too high for me to climb.

You are like a gold fish swimming in a pond, only an arm's length from the bank; yet if I try to catch you in my hand, you slip from my grasp.

You are like a snake, your skin dazzling in its bright colours, yet your tongue able to destroy a man with a single prick.

Be merciful to me, O Lord. Give me life, not death. Reach out to me, and hold me in your arms. Come down to me, and lift me up to heaven. Sustain my feeble soul with your power.

Manikka Vasahar

God, you are immortal. You do not know death. You live always. You never know that cold sleep from which a man never wakes. Your children never gather round your death-bed.

O God, you are the immortal father of our

people. Your health never fails. Your benign shadow is cast over all our actions.

You are powerful, we are powerless. You are strong, we are weak. Hear us when we call upon you. Accept the sacrifices we offer. We belong to you. Protect us as your own.

Wapokomo

Loving you, O God, brings its own reward here on earth, as well as the eternal reward of heaven. And failure to love you, even when we can offer a thousand excuses, brings its own punishment. By becoming mirrors of your love, by wearing the mask of your likeness, and by allowing you to make us perfect, we can know the joy of heaven, even while we abide here on earth. Our consciences are sullied by our many sins; cleanse them, that we may reflect your infinite brightness.

William of St Thierry

I worship you in every religion that teaches your laws and praises your glory. I worship you in every plant whose beauty reflects

your beauty. I worship you in every event
which is caused by your goodness and
kindness. I worship you in every place
where you dwell. And I worship you in
every man and woman who seeks to follow
your way of righteousness.

Zoroaster

LOVE AND COMPASSION

Jesus, how sweet is the very thought of you!
You fill my heart with joy. The sweetness of
your love surpasses the sweetness of honey.
Nothing sweeter than you can be described;
no words can express the joy of your love.
Only those who have tasted your love for
themselves can comprehend it. In your love
you listen to all my prayers, even when my
wishes are childish, my words, confused,
and my thoughts foolish. And you answer
my prayers, not according to my own
misdirected desires, which would bring only
bitter misery, but according to my real
needs, which brings me sweet joy. Thank
you, Jesus, for giving yourself to me.

Bernard of Clairvaux

Teach us to love and be loved
in perfect transparency.

Let our love be diaphanous,
lest we project
the mote in our eye
into the eye of another,

and make it a beam besides!
Let our love be transparent
lest we ever play host
to a love that is false.
Love that springs from aught but you,
love that lives in aught but you,
love that returns not to you,
is not love.

Teach us to love each and every person
as if he or she
were the only person on earth.
After all,
this is how you love:
uniquely, truly, robustly;
it's perfect, your way.
But our way,
in this poor human clay,
love creates incredible problems,
given the machismo
common that the three sexes
and most particularly
to the unlucky third...

Helder Camara

Lord, I make you a present of myself. I do not know what to do with myself. So let me make this exchange: I will place myself entirely in your hands, if you will cover my ugliness with your beauty, and tame my unruliness with your love. Put out the flames of false passion in my heart, since these flames destroy all that is true within me. Make me always busy in your service.

Lord, I want no special signs from you, nor am I looking for intense emotions in response to your love. I would rather be free of all emotion, than to run the danger of falling victim once again to false passion. Let my love for you be naked, without any emotional clothing.

Catherine of Genoa

Your light, dear God, surpasses all other light, because all light comes from you. Your fire surpasses all fire, because your fire alone burns without destroying. The flames of your fire reach into the soul, consuming the sin and selfishness that lie there. But far from damaging the soul, your fire sets it ablaze with love.

What moved you to enlighten me with your truth? The fire of your love was the reason. You loved me so much that you could not bear to see me confused and perplexed. Can I ever repay the burning love which you have given me? No, because I have nothing of my own to give. Yet you assure me that the love which you put into my soul is repayment enough. You desire only the joy of seeing me receiving your gift. What more perfect Father could there be!

Catherine of Siena

Great God, how I love you; O, how I love you!
I feel myself burning; you are the fire that burns me.
O pain, O infinitely happy pain of love!
O sweet fire! O sweet flames!
You, O sweet Lord, have set my heart ablaze.
Your fire destroys my sinful self, reducing it to ashes.
Stop, stop! I cannot pull myself away from such fire.
No, let me stay! Let the fire consume me.

Gemma Galgani

Lord, we thank thee for all the love that has been given to us, for the love of family and friends, and above all for your love poured out upon us every moment of our lives in steadfast glory. Forgive our unworthiness. Forgive the many times we have disappointed those who love us, have failed them, wearied them, saddened them. Failing them we have failed you, and in hurting them we have wounded our Saviour who for love's sake died for us. Lord, have mercy on us, and forgive. You do not fail those who love you. You do not change nor vary. Teach us your own constancy in love, your humility, selflessness and generosity. Look in pity on our small and tarnished loving, protect, foster and strengthen it, that it may be less unworthy to be offered to you and to your children. O Light of the world, teach us how to love.

Elizabeth Goudge

Lord, give me faith that tries and tests the things unseen, and assures itself of thee who art the truth, that doubt may not overwhelm nor darkness cover me; give me hope, that I

may follow the light of thy sure promises,
and lose not the way nor fall into byways;
give me love, that I may give thee myself as
thou givest; for thou, O Lord God, art the
thing that I long for; and thou art blessedness
beyond all thought and heart's desiring.

Frederick Macnutt

Just as a grain of wheat must die in the earth
in order to bring forth a rich harvest, so your
Son died on the cross to bring a rich harvest
of love. Just as the harvest of wheat must be
ground into flour to make bread, so the
suffering of your Son brings us the bread of
life. Just as bread gives our bodies strength
for our daily work, so the risen body of your
Son gives us strength to obey your laws.

Thomas Münzer

O God, whose love is without measure: out
of the depths of my own creatureliness and
yearning I call to you. Out of your own
immense depths of power and mystery you
call to me. Enable me to enter into the
beginnings of the secrets of your love, and

let the poor stream of my life flow into the
immensity of your Being.
Brother Ramon

May you be blessed, Lord, that from such
filthy mud, as I, you make water so clear
that it can be served at your table. May you
be praised for having raised up a worm so
vile.

With what skill you have re-fashioned my
soul from miserable ugliness to divine
beauty! With what gently coaxing you have
lured me from the false pleasures of sin to
the true joy of your love! And yet with what
force you have snapped the chains of sin,
and freed my soul to adore you!
Teresa of Avila

Majestic sovereign, timeless wisdom
Your kindness melts my hard, cold soul.
Handsome lover, selfless giver,
Your beauty fills my dull, sad eyes.
I am yours, you made me.
I am yours, you called me
I am yours, you saved me.

I am yours, you loved me.
I will never leave your presence.
Give me death, give me life.
Give me sickness, give me health.
Give me honour, give me shame.
Give me weakness, give me strength
I will have whatever you give.

Teresa of Avila

My God, everywhere your love is misunderstood and cast aside. The hearts upon which you are ready to lavish your love turn away towards earthly pleasures instead, as if happiness could be found in more material attachments. They refuse to throw themselves into your arms and accept the gift of your infinite love. Must this rejected love of yours remain shut up in your own heart? If yonly you could find yourself souls ready to offer themselves as victims, to be burnt up in the fire of your love! You would lose no time in satisfying their desire. Thus you would find a welcome outlet for the pent-up force of your great devotion.

Jesus, grant me the happiness of being such a victim, burnt up in the fire of your divine love.

Thérèse of Lisieux

My Jesus, from all eternity you were pleased to give yourself to us in love. And you planted within us a deep spiritual desire that can only be satisfied by yourself.

I may go from here to the other end of the world, from one country to another, from riches to greater riches, from pleasure to pleasure, and still I shall not be content. All the world cannot satisfy the immortal soul. It would be like trying to feed a starving man with a single grain of wheat.

We can only be satisfied by setting our hearts, imperfect as they are, on you. We are made to love you; you created us as your lovers.

It sometimes happens that the more we know a neighbour, the less we love him. But with you it is quite the opposite. The more we know you, the more we love you. Knowledge of you kindles such a fire in our souls that we have no energy left for worldly desires.

My Jesus, how good it is to love you. Let me be like your disciples on Mount Tabor, seeing nothing else but you. Let us be like two bosom friends, neither of whom can ever bear to offend the other.

Jean-Baptiste Marie Vianney

MERCY

Lord Jesus, you have invited me to your banquet table, though I deserve to be thrown into the dungeon. So I accept your invitation in fear and trembling, encouraged only by your mercy and goodness.

My soul and body are defiled by so many sinful deeds. My tongue and my heart have run wild without restraint, causing misery to others and shame to myself. My soul bleeds with the wounds of wrong-doing, and my body is like a temple of Satan. If I was to come before you as my judge, you could only condemn me to eternal torment, for that is what I deserve.

Yet I come before you, not as a judge, but as a saviour. I depend not on your justice, but on your mercy. As you look upon the wretched creature that I am, I ask that your eyes be filled with compassion and forgiveness. And as I sit at your table, I beg you to renew within me a spirit of holiness, that I may be worthy to share your supper.

Ambrose of Milan

We come before you, source of all being,
As sinners.
We have betrayed you.
We saw a great lie raise its head,
And we did not honour the truth.
We saw our brethren in direst need,
And we feared only for our own safety.

We come before you, source of all mercy,
As confessors do our sins.
After the ferment of these terrible times,
Send us times of assurance.
After wandering so long in darkness,
Let us walk in the light of the sun.
After the falsehood of the current way,
Build a road for us by your Word.

And until you wipe out our guilt,
Lord, make us patient.

Dietrich Bonhoeffer

Merciful Lord, it does not surprise me that
you forget completely the sins of those who
repent. I am not surprised that you remain
faithful to those who hate and revile you.

The mercy which pours forth from you fills the whole world.

It was by your mercy that we were created, and by your mercy that you redeemed us by sending your Son. Your mercy is the light in which sinners find you and good people come back to you. Your mercy is everywhere, even in the depths of Hell where you offer to forgive the tortured souls. Your justice is constantly tempered with mercy, so you refuse to punish us as we deserve. O mad lover! It was not enough for you to take on our humanity; you had to die for us as well.

Catherine of Siena

O Lord, I most humbly acknowledge and confess that I have understood sin, by understanding thy laws and judgements; but have gone against thy known and revealed will. Thou hast set up many candlesticks, and kindled many lamps in me; but I have either blown them out , or carried them to guide me in forbidden ways. Thou hast given me a desire of knowledge, and some means to it, and some possession of it; and I have arm'd myself with thy weapons against thee. Yet, O God, have mercy upon me, for thine own sake have mercy upon me. Let not sin and me be able to exceed thee, nor to defraud thee, nor to frustrate thy purposes. But let me, in spite of me, be of so much use to thy glory, that by thy mercy to my sin, other sinners may see how much sin thou canst pardon.

John Donne

When we see dark grey clouds forming in the sky, we fear a mighty storm. In the same way when we see the darkness of our sin, we fear the storm of your wrath. But just as in truth rain brings new life to the earth, so you rain down mercy on our sinful souls, bringing forgiveness and peace. Be to us always like a mighty storm, raining down upon us the abundant waters of your mercy.

Gilbert of Hoyland

Ah my dear angry Lord,
Since thou dost love, yet strike;
Cast down, yet help afford;

Sure I will do the like.
I will complain, yet praise;
I will bewail, approve;
And all my sour-sweet days
I will lament, and love.

George Herbert

Merciful God, we know that we deserve to
have your anger poured out upon us; yet in
your infinite love you have chosen instead to
pour out the grace of your Holy Spirit. May
your Spirit so enlighten our hearts, that we
may show the same merciful love to others
that you have shown to us.

Thomas Münzer

Helper of men who turn to you,
Light of men in the dark,
Creator of all that grows from seed,
Promoter of all spiritual growth,
Have mercy, Lord, on me.
And make me a temple fit for you.
Do not look too closely at my sins,
For if you are quick to notice my faults
I shall not dare to appear before you.

In your great mercy,
In your boundless love,
Wash away my sins
By the hand of Jesus Christ,
Your only child, the chief healer of souls.

Prayers from Papyri

PEACE

O God, which art author of peace, and lover
of concord, in knowledge of whom standeth
our eternal life, whose service is perfect
freedom: defend us, thy humble servants, in
all assaults of our enemies, that we, surely
trusting in the defence, may not fear the
power of any adversaries.

The Book of Common Prayer

O God, from whom all holy desires, all good
counsels, and all just works proceed: Give
unto thy servants that peace which the
world cannot give; that both our hearts may
be set to obey thy commandments, and also
that by thee we, being defended from the
fear of our enemies, may pass our time in
rest and quietness.

The Book of Common Prayer

O God, we know that the enemies of your
church are constantly seeking to provoke
you into acts of cruelty, in order to blacken
your honour. We beg and beseech that you

will tame their wild hearts. May their rage subside and bring peace to their souls. May their minds, clouded by the darkness which their sins produce, repent and turn towards the bright light of your forgiveness. Now they thirst for our blood because we are your loyal followers; may they instead thirst for our love and our prayers.

Cyprian of Carthage

O God, grant that I may practise such temperance in meat, drink, and sleep, and all bodily enjoyments, as may fit me for the duties to which thou shalt call me. And by thy blessing procure me freedom of thought and quietness of mind, that I may so serve thee in this short and frail life, that I may be received by thee at my death to everlasting happiness. Take not, O Lord, thy Holy Spirit from me, deliver me not up to vain fears, but have mercy on me.

Samuel Johnson

O Lord Jesus Christ, who didst say that in thee we may have peace, and hast bidden us to be of good cheer, since thou hast overcome the world: give us ears to hear and faith to receive thy word; that in all the tensions and confusion of this present time, with mind serene and steadfast purpose, we may continue to abide in thee.

Frederick Macnutt

O God, through the death of your Son you reconciled us one to another, drawing us together in the bond of peace. In times of trouble and adversity, may your peace sustain us, calming our fretful and anxious hearts, and saving us from all hateful and violent activities.

Mozarabic Sacramentary

When thou commandest me to sing it seems that my heart would break with pride; and I look to thy face, and tears come to my eyes. All that is harsh and dissonant in my life melts into one sweet harmony – and my adoration spreads wings like a glad bird on its flight across the sea. I know thou takest pleasure in my singing. I know that only as a singer I come before thy presence. I touch by the edge of the far spreading wing of my song thy feet which I could never aspire to reach. Drunk with the joy of singing I forget myself and call thee friend who art my lord.

Rabindranath Tagore

GRACE

O King of glory, and Lord of valour, our
warrior and our peace, may you win
victories in the world through us your
servants, for without you we can do nothing.
May your compassion go before us and
come behind us; be with
us at our beginnings, and at our endings.
May your will be done in everything we
do, for you are our salvation, our glory and
our joy.

Alcuin of York

Lord Christ, we pray thy mercy on our table
  spread,
And what thy gentle hands have given thy
  men
Let it by thee be blessed: whate'er we have
Came from thy lavish heart and gentle hand,
And all that's good is thine, for thou art
  good.
And ye that eat, give thanks for it to Christ,
And let the words ye utter be only peace,
For Christ loved peace: it was himself that
  said,

Peace I give unto you, my peace I leave with
  you.
Grant that our own may be a generous hand
Breaking the bread for all poor men, sharing
  the food.
chirst shall receive the bread thou gavest his
  poor,
And shall not tarry to give thee reward.

Alcuin of York

O Lord, our heavenly Father, almighty and
ever living God, which hast safely brought
us to the beginning of this day: defend us in
the same with thy mighty power; and grant
that this day we fall into no sin, neither run
into any kind of danger, but that all our
doings may be ordered by thy governance,
to do always that is righteous in thy sight.

The Book of Common Prayer

Lord, when the sense of thy sweet grace
Sends up my soul to seek thy face,
Thy blessed eyes breed such desire,
I die in one's delicious fire.
O love, I am thy sacrifice.

Be still triumphant, blessed eyes.
Still shine on me, fair suns! that I
Still may behold, though still I die.
                              Richard Crashaw

By the grace of your name
May humanity find itself lifted higher and
  higher.
In your dispensation O Lord,
Let virtue reign in every human heart.
                              Nanak

Lord, we are rivers running to thy sea,
Our waves and ripples all derived from thee:
A nothing we should have, a nothing be,
Except for thee.
Sweet are the waters of thy shoreless seas,
Make sweet our waters that make haste to
  thee;
Pour in thy sweetness, that ourselves may be
Sweetness to thee.
                              Christina Rossetti

Thou hast made me endless, such is thy
pleasure. This frail vessel thou emptiest

149

again and again, and fillest it ever with fresh
life. This little flute of a reed thou hast
carried over hills and dales, and hast
breathed through it melodies eternally new.
At the immortal touch of thy hands my little
heart loses it limits in joy and gives birth to
utterance ineffable. Thy infinite gifts come to
me only on these very small hands of mine.
Ages pass, and still thou pourest, and still
there is room to fill.

Rabindranath Tagore

O Almighty God who fillest all things with
plenty, teach me to use thy creatures soberly
and temperately, that I may not, with loads
of meat or drinks, make my spirit unapt for
the performance of my duty, or my body
healthless, or my affections sensual and
unholy. In the strength of thy provisions
may I cheerfully and actively and diligently
serve thee; that I may worthily feast at thy
table here, and through thy grace, be
admitted to thy table hereafter.

Jeremy Taylor

O Almighty God, Father and Lord of all the
creatures, by secret and undiscernible ways
bringing good out of evil: give me wisdom
from above; teach me to be content in all
changes of person and condition, to be
temperate in prosperity, and in adversity to
be meek, patient, and resigned; and to look
through the cloud, in the meantime doing
my duty with an unwearied diligence, and
an undisturbed resolution.

Jeremy Taylor

Dear Lord, you give so much, while I give so
little. I should give up everything for you,
trusting you to care for my every need. Yet I
fail, I fail, I fail – I could say it a thousand
times – I fail to give up everything for you. I
hate even to continue living in the shame of
my failure, because I know that the only
purpose in life is to offer back to you all that
you have given to us. How many
imperfections I see in myself! I would like to
be knocked unconscious so that I am no
longer aware of my wickedness. Lord, knock
your grace into me, that I may truly be good.

Teresa of Avila

King of heaven, you have revealed your wonder even to someone as vile as me. You have taken from them the false joy of earthly pleasures, and given me instead the true joy of your heavenly love. You have taken me into your heavenly family, treating me as a beloved child. And I cling to you as a small child clings to its mother. I will never let go; I will always stay in your presence.

King of heaven, you have showered your wealth even onto someone as undeserving as me. You have taken from them any desire for the perishable riches of earth, and given me instead only the desire for the imperishable wealth of heaven. You have taken me into your royal court, treating me as the chief steward of your spiritual treasures. I bow before you as a servant bows to his master. I will never cease to adore you; I will always strive to serve you.

Manikka Vasahar

Almighty Lord, if we offer you a devoted mind and heart, you will offer to us every blessing on earth and in heaven.

Atharva Veda

PROVIDENCE

You speak, Lord to all men in general
through general events. Revolutions are
simply the tides of your Providence, which
stir up storms and tempests in people's
minds. You speak to men in particular
through particular events as signals of your
loving guidance, people see nothing else but
blind chance and human decision. They find
objections to everything you say. They wish
to add to or subtract from your world. They
wish to change and reform it.

Teach me, dear Lord, to read clearly this
book of life. I wish to be like a simple child,
accepting your word regardless of whether I
understand your purposes. It is enough for
me that you speak.

Jean-Pierre de Caussade

O Unknown Love! We are inclined to think
that your marvels are over, and that all we
can do is to copy the ancient Scriptures that
quote your words from the past. We fail to
see that your inexhaustible action is the
source of new thoughts, new sufferings,

new actions, new leaders, new prophets, new apostles, new saints, who have no need to copy each other's lives and writings, but live in perpetual self-abandonment to your operations. We hear perpetually of the 'early centuries' and the 'times of the saints.' What a way to talk! Are not all times and all events successive results of your grace, pouring itself forth on all instants of time, filling them and sanctifying them? Your divine action will continue until the world ends to shed its glory on those souls who abandon themselves to your providence without reserve.

Jean-Pierre de Caussade

Lord, may your kingdom come into my heart to sanctify me, nourish me and purify me. How insignificant is the passing moment to the eye without faith! But how important each moment is to the eye enlightened by faith! How can we deem insignificant anything which has been caused by you? Every moment and every event is guided by you, and so contains your infinite greatness.

So, Lord, I glorify you in everything that
happens to me. In whatever manner you
make me live and die, I am content. Events
please me for their own sake, regardless of
the consequences, because your action lies
behind them. Everything is heaven to me,
because all my moments manifest your love.

Jean-Pierre de Caussade

I do not eat, Lord, just because I am hungry,
nor merely to give me pleasure. No, I eat
because, in your providence, you have
created me with the need for food.

When I must turn to a friend for help, I
recognise that you have created man to help,
comfort and encourage each other. And
since this is your wish, I will turn to those
whose friendship is your gift to me.

When I have good reason to be afraid of
something, I recognise that you want me to
be afraid, in order that I should take suitable
steps to avoid danger. So I shall act on my
fear, according to your will. If fear becomes
excessive, I can turn to you, knowing that as
your child I can nestle in your loving arms.

Thus, Lord, I try to do the right thing. And

when I have done all I can, I know that whatever happens is an expression of your will.
Francis of Sales

How brief is our span of life compared with
the time since you created the universe. How
tiny we are compared with the enormity of
your universe. How trivial are our concerns
compared with the complexity of your
universe. How stupid we are compared with
the genius of your creation. Yet during every
minute and every second of our lives you
are present, within and around us. You give
your whole and undivided attention to each
and every one of us. Our concerns are your
concerns. And you are infinitely patient with
our stupidity. I thank you with all my heart
– knowing that my thanks are worthless
compared with your greatness.
Fulbert of Chartres

Teach me, my God and King,
    In all things thee to see,
And what I do in anything,
    To do it as for thee:

Not rudely, as a beast,
  To run into an action;
But still to make thee prepossess
  And give it his perfection.

A man that looks on glass,
  On it may stay his eye;
Or if he pleaseth, through it pass,
  And then heav'n espy.

All may of thee partake:
  Nothing can be so mean,
Which with this tincture (for thy sake)
  Will not grow bright and clean

A servant with this clause
  Makes drudgery divine:
Who sweeps a room as for thy laws,
  Makes that and th' action fine.

This is the famous stone
  That turneth all to gold:
For that which God doth touch and own
  Cannot for less be told.

George Herbert

O Lord, fulfil thy Will
Be the days of few or many, good or ill:
Prolong them, to suffice
For offering up ourselves thy sacrifice;
Shorten them if thou wilt,
To make in righteousness an end of guilt,
Yea, they will not be long
To souls who learn to sing a patient song:
yea, short they will not be
To souls on tiptoe to flee home to these.
O Lord, fulfil thy Will:
Make thy Will ours, and keep us patient still
Be the days few or many, good or ill.

Christina Rossetti

O Almighty God, infinite and eternal, thou
art in the consciences of all men. Teach me to
walk always as in thy presence, to fear thy
majesty, to reverence thy wisdom: that I may
never dare to commit any indecency in the
eye of my Lord and my Judge; that I,
expressing the belief of thy presence here,
may feel the effects of it in eternal glory.

Jeremy Taylor

GUIDANCE

Steer the ship of my life, good Lord, to your
quiet harbour, where I can be safe from the
storms of sin and conflict. Show me the
course I should take. Renew in me the gift of
discernment, so that I can always see the
right direction in which I should go. And
give me the strength and the courage to
choose the right course, even when the sea is
rough and the waves are high, knowing that
through enduring hardship and danger in
your name we shall find comfort and peace.

Basil of Caesarea

Be kind to your little children, Lord. Be a
gentle teacher, patient with our weakness
and stupidity. And give us the strength and
discernment to do what you tell us, and so
grow in your likeness.

May we all live in the peace that comes
from you. May we journey towards your
city, sailing through the waters of sin
untouched by the waves, borne serenely
along by the Holy Spirit. Night and day may
we give you praise and thanks, because you

have shown us that all things belong to you,
and all blessings are gifts from you. To you,
the essence of wisdom, the foundation of
truth, be the glory for evermore.

Clement of Alexandria

Lord, I pray that you may be a lamp for me
in the darkness. Touch my soul and kindle a
fire within it, that it may burn brightly and
give light to my life. Thus my body may
truly become your temple, lit by your
perpetual flame burning on the altar of my
heart. And may the light within me shine on
my brethren that it may drive away the
darkness of ignorance and sin from them
also. Thus together let us be lights to the
world, manifesting the beauty of your gospel
to all around us.

Columbanus

Lord, you are here,
Lord, you are there.
You are wherever we go.
Lord, you guide us,

Lord, you protect us.
You are wherever we go.
Lord, we need you,
Lord, we trust you,
You are wherever we go.
Lord, we love you,
Lord we praise you
You are wherever we go.

Dinka

May your Spirit guide my mind,
Which is so often dull and empty.
Let my thoughts always be on you,
And let me see you in all things.

May your Spirit quicken my soul,
Which is so often listless and lethargic.
Let my soul be awake to your presence,
And let me know you in all things.

May your Spirit melt my heart,
Which is so often cold and indifferent.
Let my heart be warmed by your love,
And let me feel you in all things.

Johann Freylinghausen

I see man walketh in a vain shadow and disquieteth himself in vain; they are pitiful pleasures he enjoyeth while he forgetteth thee. I am as vain, make me more wise. O, let me see heaven and I know I shall never envy nor follow them. My times are in thine hands; I am no better than my fathers, a stranger on earth. As I speak of them, so the next, yea, this generation shall speak of me as one that was. My life is a bubble, a smoke, a shadow, a thought; I know it hath no abiding in this thoroughfare. O, suffer me not so mad as while I pass on the way I should forget the end. It is that other life that I must trust to. With thee it is that I shall continue.

Joseph Hall

Lead, kindly light, amid the encircling
  gloom,
    Lead thou me on;
The night is dark, and I am far from home;
    Lead thou me on.
Keep thou my feet; I do not ask to see
The distant scene: one step enough for me.

I was not ever thus, nor prayed that thou
    Shouldst lead me on;

I loved to choose and see my path; but now
    Lead thou me on.
I loved the garish day, and, spite fears,
Pride ruled my will: remember not past years.

So long thy power hath blest me, sure it still
    Will lead me on
O'er moor and fen, o'er crag and torrent, till
    The night is gone,
And with the morn those angel faces smile
Which I have loved long since, and lost
    awhile.

John Henry Newman

Grant that we here before thee may be set
free from the fear of vicissitude and the fear
of death, may finish what remains before us
of our course without dishonour to
ourselves or hurt to others; and when the
day comes, may die in peace. Deliver us
from fear and favour: from mean hopes and
cheap pleasures. Have mercy on each in his
deficiency; let him be not cast down;
Support the stumbling on the way, and give
at last rest to the weary.

Robert Louis Stevenson

How is it, my God, that you have given me this hectic busy life when I have so little time to enjoy your presence. Throughout the day people are waiting to speak with me, and even at meals I have to continue talking to people about their needs and problems. During sleep itself I am still thinking and dreaming about the multitiude of concerns that surround me. I do all this not for my own sake, but for yours. To me my present pattern of life is a torment; I only hope that for you it is truly a sacrifice of love. I know that you are constantly beside me, yet I am usually so busy that I ignore you. If you want me to remain so busy, please force me to think about and love you even in the midst of such hectic activity. If you do not want me so busy, please release me from it, showing how others can take over my responsibilities.

Teresa of Avila

The
human condition

DEATH AND LIFE

Since no one, Lord, can desire more for
another man than he wishes for himself, I
ask you not to separate me when I am dead
from those who were so dear to me while I
lived. I beg that where I am, they too may be
with me. As I have not been able to see
much of them here on earth, let me enjoy
their company in heaven for ever. I beseech
you, God most high, to grant a speedy
resurrection to these children whom I love
so much.

Ambrose of Milan

You watch over the insignificant, Lord, and
keep them humble. Protect all who put their
trust in you. Give rest to all who die in faith,
returning their souls whence they came.
May they not feel the sting of death. Instead
let them know that death is the death of sin,
and thence the beginning of eternal life.

Ambrose of Milan

O God, we thy creatures try to evade the fact of death, and to keep it out of mind, yet in our deeper moments we know it is a warning note, urging us so to die every day to all selfishness and sin, that when the times comes for our final migration, we may take death in our stride because life is so strong within us, as it was in him who was so manifestly thy true Son and so convincingly the prototype of thy finished humanity, even Jesus Christ, thy Son, our brother.

George Appleton

I beseech you, good Jesus, that as you have graciously granted to me here on earth to enjoy the sweetness of your wisdom and truth, so at death you will bring me into your presence, that I may see the beauty of your face, and listen to your voice which is the source of all wisdom and truth.

Bede

O God, early in the morning I cry to you.
Help me to pray
And concentrate my thoughts on you:

I cannot do this alone.
In me there is darkness,
But with you there is light;
I am lonely, but you do not leave me;
I am feeble in heart, but with you there is
   help;
I am restless, but with you there is peace.
In me there is bitterness, but with you there
   is patience;
I do not understand your ways,
But you know the way for me . . .

Restore me to liberty,
And enable me so to live now
That I may answer before you and before
   me.
Lord, whatever this day may bring,
Your name be praised.

Dietrich Bonhoeffer

O King of the Tree of Life,
The blossoms on the branches are your
   people,
The singing birds are your angels,
The whispering breeze is your Spirit.

O King of the Tree of Life,
May the blossoms bring forth the sweetest
  fruit,
May the birds sing out the highest praise
May your Spirit cover all with his gentle
  breath.

Celtic Prayers

Wait for me, King of Heaven, until I am
pure, fit to live in your house.
Wait for me, Mary's Son, until I am old, wise
from the passing of years.
When a young boy is carried off before his
years of playing are over, no one knows
what greatness he has missed; only in
adulthood comes the full bloom of our gifts.
A calf should not be killed before it is full-
grown, nor a pig slaughtered when it is still
sucking at the sow's breast.
A bough should not be cut until it has
flowered, nor a field harvested until the
grain is full.
The sun should not set at midday, nor rise at
midnight.
Keep my soul here on earth, for it is like soft,

unforced clay, not ready to be received by you.
Yet even if you cut me off in my youth, I shall not complain, but continue to worship you.

Celtic Prayers

I give you thanks, my King, for the care you have lavished upon me.
I have for six months been lying on my bed, my body racked by disease; I am a prisoner, held in chains by my illness.
My strength is gone, from my head to my feet I can barely move; my weakness is like fetters holding me down.
I am like a blind man unable to see the world around me; for six months I have seen only the walls of my hut.
You have nailed me to my cross; this sickness is my crucifixion.
And so I give you thanks, my King, for bringing me joyfully to judgement.
Tomorrow I shall die, and see you face to face; tomorrow your lash on my body shall cease, and I shall be at peace.

If now my body is shrouded by clouds of
  darkness, my soul basks in warm light; if
  now my eyes are filled with bitter tears, my
  soul can taste the sweetest honey.
I am like a mouse, caught in a trap and
  shaken in the claws of a cat; tomorrow I
  shall be as free as the wind.
My present pains are as nothing compared
  to the enormity of my sin; your mercy is
  infinite and eternal.

Celtic Prayers

One day my soul must depart from this
body. When will it be? In winter or summer?
In town or country? During the day or
night? Suddenly or with warning? Due to
illness or an accident? Shall I have a chance
to confess my sins? Shall there be a priest to
assist me? I know none of these things. One
thing only is certain, that I will die, and
sooner than I would like.

  Dear God, take me into your arms on that
most important day. May all other days be
sad, if only that day may be happy. I tremble
with fear at the prospect, yet I know that
you, and you alone, can save me.

Set my whole heart on your promise of
heaven. Guide my feet in your ways, O
Lord, that I may walk the straight path
towards eternal life. Let me cast off
everything that holds me back on my
journey there, so that all my strength may be
directed towards that goal.

Francis of Sales

I know, O God, that the time appointed by
you for my death is almost here. I know now
that soon I shall appear before you to be
judged. And I know that I am a great sinner.
I have broken all your holy commandments.
I have frequently failed to love you, and
strayed from the footsteps of Jesus. I have at
times closed my heart to the guidance of the
Holy Spirit. I have often missed
opportunities to help my neighbour, because
I have been so pre-occupied with my own
wants and desires.

Yet at this hour of crisis I feel bold enough
to beg your forgiveness. Yes, I am fearful of
your judgement. But I am also confident of
your mercy. In that confidence I ask you to
blot out my sinfulness, and remember only

those times – few as they are – when I have been faithful to you, obeying your commandments and following the teachings of your Son. Lord, I know I am not fit for Heaven; make me fit.

Johann Starck

SUFFERING AND JOY

Lord, let me welcome all the pain and suffering that comes to me, for pain and suffering are sent by you. Ever since you enlightened me, thirty-six years ago, I have sought to suffer, both spiritually and physically. And yet because I have desired suffering, all suffering has seemed sweet and pleasant, knowing that you are its source. Now that I am near to death, and my whole body is in agony from head to toe, I find myself wondering if I can endure this final encounter with pain. I know that you rule over my pain, and will bring relief when I am ready to be received into your heavenly kingdom. So even in the midst of this agony, I cannot really say that I am suffering. You make all things bearable, filling my heart with inexpressible joy.

Catherine of Genoa

Thou hast made me, and shall thy work
  decay?
Repair me now, for now mine end doth
  haste,

I run to death, and death meets me as fast,
And all my pleasures are like yesterday;
I dare not move my dim eyes any way,
Despair behind, and death before doth cast
Such terror, and my feebled flesh doth waste
By sin in it, which it t'wards hell doth weigh;
Only thou'rt above, and when towards thee
By thy leave I can look, I rise again;
But our old subtle foe so tempteth me
That not one hour mys self I can sustain;
Thy grace may wing me to prevent his art,
And thou like Adamant draw mine iron
    heart.   *John Donne*

Batter my heart, three person'd God; for, you
As yet but knock, breathe, shine, and seek to
    mend;
That I may rise, and stand, o'erthrow me,
    and bend
Your force, to break, blow, burn and make
    me new,
I, like an usurped town, to another due,
Labour to admit you, but Oh, to no end,
Reason your viceroy in me, me should
    defend,
But is captiv'd, and proves weak or untrue.

Yet dearly I love you, and would be loved
fain,
But am betroth'd unto your enemy:
Divorce me, untie, or break that knot again,
Take me to you, imprison me, for I
Except you enthrall me, never shall be free,
Nor ever chaste, except you ravish me.

John Donne

O my God, you alone can perceive the
depths of our weakness; and you alone can
heal us. Turn our eyes continually to you,
our all-powerful Father, and to your Son,
our example in courageous suffering. He
was nailed to the cross, so we might learn
that suffering can be turned into a blessing.
We long for physical comfort and bodily
pleasure; so when we gaze on your Son, his
body wracked with pain, we shudder at
such a terrifying sight. Yet when we see him
rise again in glory, we know that the nails
which fixed him to the cross were also used
to fashion the gate of eternal life.

Help us never again to fear suffering, but
only to fear sin. Give us the courage to
embrace such suffering as you send us, in

the sure and certain knowledge of your
eternal bliss.

Fenelon

Lord, how much juice you can squeeze from
  a single grape.
How much water you can draw from a
  single well.
How great a fire you can kindle from a tiny
  spark.
How great a tree you can grow from a tiny seed.
My soul is so dry that by itself it cannot pray;
Yet you can squeeze from it the juice of a
  thousand prayers.
My soul is so parched that by itself it cannot love;
Yet you can draw from it boundless love for you
  and for my neighbour.
My soul is so cold that by itself it has no joy;
Yet you can light the fire of heavenly joy within
  me.
My soul is so feeble that by itself it has no faith;
Yet by your power my faith grows to a great
  height.
Thank you for prayer, for love, for joy, for faith;
Let me always be prayerful, loving, joyful,
  faithful.

Guigo the Carthusian

Ah my dear angry Lord,
Since thou dost love, yet strike;
Cast down, yet help afford;
Sure I will complain, yet praise;
I will bewail, approve;
And all my sour-sweet days
I will lament, and love.

George Herbert

You, Lord, are all that I have, and you give
me all that I need; my future is in your
hands. How wonderful are your gifts to me;
how good they are.

I bless you, Lord, because you guide me.
In the night also you instruct my heart. I am
constantly aware of your presence; and,
knowing that you are near, I cannot be
shaken from my faith.

So my soul is joyful and I feel completely
secure, under your protection. I am
confident that you shall never abandon me.
You show me the path of life, which leads to
eternal bliss.

Book of Psalms

Lord, how can I endure this life of sorrow,
unless you strengthen me with your mercy
and grace? Do not turn your face from me.
Do not withdraw your consolation from me,
lest my soul becomes like a waterless desert.
Teach me, O Lord, to do your will, and to
live humbly. You alone know me perfectly,
seeing into my soul. You alone can give
lasting peace and joy.

Thomas à Kempis

SICKNESS AND HEALING

Just as day declines to evening, so often after
some little pleasure my heart declines into
depression. Everything seems dull, every
action feels like a burden. If anyone speaks, I
scarcely listen. If anyone knocks, I scarcely
hear. My heart is as hard as flint. Then I go
out into the field to meditate, to read the
holy Scriptures, and I write down my deepest thoughts in a letter to you. And suddenly
your grace, dear Jesus, shatters the darkness
with daylight, lifts the burden, relieves the
tension. Soon tears follow sighs, and
heavenly joy floods over me with the tears.
Aelred of Rievaulx

O Holy Spirit who dost delve into all things,
even the deep things of God
and the deep things of man,
we pray thee to penetrate the springs of
  personality
of all who are sick in mind,
to bring them cleansing, healing, and unity.
Sanctify all memory, dispel all fear,
bring them to love thee

with all their mind and will,
that they may be made whole
and glorify thee for ever.
We ask this in the name of him
who cast out devils and healed men's minds,
even Jesus Christ our Lord.

George Appleton

Most powerful Lord, beneath whose wings
we find protection and shelter, you are
invisible and untouchable, like the night and
like the air. I appear before you, stammering
with nervous uncertainty, as one who has
stumbled and lost his way. I am afraid that
my wrong-doing has provoked your wrath
and aroused your indignation against me.
For that is the only explanation I can find for
the terrible sickness that has fallen upon my
family. The misery of my children is surely
the consequence of my wickedness.

Lord, do with my body whatever pleases.
Heap upon me whatever diseases I deserve.
Do not spare me any suffering or any
indignity. Let me bear the punishment for
my own actions. And so let my children be

restored to health and happiness, that they may stand upright and follow your path of righteousness. Let me die, that they may live.

Aztec

O Lord, holy Father, creator of the universe, author of its laws, you can bring the dead back to life, and heal those who are sick. We pray for our sick brother that he may feel your hand upon him, renewing his body and refreshing his soul. Show to him the affection in which you hold all your creatures.

Dimma

O God, you rule over your creation with tenderness, offering fresh hope in the midst of the most terrible misery. We pray for our brother whose soul is blackened by despair, infusing him with the pure light of your love. As he curses the day he was born and yearns for oblivion, reveal to him the miracle of new birth which shall prepare for the joys of heaven.

Dimma

Lord Jesus Christ, you are the only source of
health for the living, and you promise
eternal life to the dying. I entrust myself to
your holy will. If you wish me to stay longer
in this world, I pray that you will heal me of
my present sickness. If you wish me to leave
this world, I readily lay aside this mortal
body, in the sure hope of receiving an
immortal body which shall enjoy everlasting
health. I ask only that you relieve me of pain,
that whether I live or I die, I may rest
peaceful and contented.

Erasmus

Christ, give me strength; your servant is not
  well.
The tongue that praised you is made silent,
Struck dumb by the pain of sickness.
I cannot bear not to sing your praises.
O, make me well again, make me whole,
That I may again proclaim your greatness.
Do not forsake me, I beseech you.
Let me return now to your service.

Gregory of Nazianzus

CONFLICT AND RECONCILIATION

Christ, why do you allow wars and
massacres on earth? By what mysterious
judgement do you allow innocent people to
be cruelly slaughtered? I cannot know. I can
only find assurance in the promise that your
people will find peace in heaven, where no-
one makes war. As gold is purified by fire,
so you purify souls by these bodily tribula-
tions, making them ready to be received
above the stars in your heavenly home.

Alcuin of York

My good Lord,
I long to pray to you for my friends,
But I am held back by my sins.
Since I stand in such need of grace myself,
How can I dare ask for grace for others?
I anxiously seek intercession on my own
  behalf.
Yet even so I shall be so bold
As to intercede for others.
You commend me to pray for my friends,
And love prompts me to do so.
So I pray to you, good and gracious God,

For those who love me for your sake
And whom I love in you.
If my prayer does not deserve to be
  answered,
Please love them for their own sakes,
For you are the source of all love.
And make them love you with all their
  hearts
So that they will speak and do
Only that which pleases you.
My prayer is but a cold affair, Lord,
Because my love burns with such a small
  flame.
Yet you who are rich in mercy
Will bestow your grace not according to my
  prayers
But according to the infinite warmth of your
  love.

Anselm of Canterbury

Almighty and tender Lord Jesus Christ,
Just as I have asked you to love my friends
So I ask the same for my enemies.
You alone, Lord, are mighty.
You alone are merciful.

Whatever you make me desire for my
  enemies,
Give it to them.
And give the same back to me.
If I ever ask for them anything
Which is outside your perfect rule of love,
Whether through weakness, ignorance or
  malice,
Good Lord, do not give it to them
And do not give it back to me.
You who are the true light, lighten their
  darkness.
You who are the whole truth, correct their
  errors.
You who are, give life to their souls.
Tender Lord Jesus,
Let me not be a stumbling-block to them
Nor a rock of offence.
My sin is sufficient to me, without harming
  others.
I, a slave to sin,
Beg your mercy on my fellow-slaves.
Let them be reconciled with you,
And through you reconciled to me.

                              Anselm of Canterbury

Most powerful Lord, under whose empire
we live, you are invisible and untouchable,
like the night and like the air. The ground is
now shaking, as warriors stamp their feet in
fury at their enemy. The earth is opening her
throat, ready to receive the blood which is
spilt in the heat of battle. Even the wild
animals run away, terrified of the coming
slaughter.

Lord, you alone know who will die and
who will live, who will collapse in defeat
and who will rise in victory. We pray that
those who fall in battle may die with honour,
and ascend to you to live among the heroes.
May they share in your eternal glory and
savour your eternal sweetness.   *Aztec*

O God, who has ordained that all men
should live and work together as brethren,
remove, we humbly beseech you, from those
who are now at variance, all spirit of strife
and all occasion for bitterness that, seeking
only what is just and equal, they may ever
continue in brotherly union and concord.
Lead us out of the night of this conflict into

the day of justice. Give us grace to be instruments of the kingdom of love and justice in the affairs of mankind; and patience in dealing with all the sins and selfishness of men, and humility in recognizing our own, that we may judge wisely between a man and his brother, between nations and peoples; and, by composing their differences, build them up into a true community of nations.

Reinhold Niebuhr

We pray for all who have some vision of your will, despite the confusions and betrayals of human sin, that they may humbly and resolutely plan for and fashion the foundations of a just peace between men, even while they seek to preserve what is fair and just among us against the threat of malignant power. Grant us grace to see what we can do, but also to know what are the limits of our powers, so that courage may feed on trust in you, who are able to rule and overrule the angry passions of men and to make the wrath of men to praise you.

Reinhold Niebuhr

Take all hate from my heart, O God, and
teach me how to take it from the hearts of
others. Open my eyes and show me what
things in our society make it easy for hatred
to flourish and hard for us to conquer it.
Then help me to try to change these things.

And so open my eyes and my ears that I
may this coming day be able to do some
work of peace for you.

Alan Paton

Help me, O Lord, to be more loving. Help
me, O Lord, not to be afraid to love the
outcast, the leper, the unmarried pregnant
woman, the traitor to the State, the man out
of prison. Help me by my love to restore the
faith of the disillusioned, the disappointed,
the early bereaved. Help me by my love to
be the witness of your love.

And may I this coming day be able to do
some work of peace for you.

Alan Paton

Lord, teach me the meaning of your
commandment to love our enemies, and
help me to obey it. Make me the instrument

of your love, which is not denied to the hungry, the sick, the prisoner, the enemy. Teach me to hate division, and not to seek after it. But teach me also to stand up for those things that I believe to be right, no matter what the consequences may be.

Alan Paton

O God, we thank thee for this universe, our great home; for its vastness and its riches, and for the manifoldness of the life which teems upon it and of which we are part. We praise thee for the arching sky and the blessed winds, for the driving clouds, and the constellations on high. We praise thee for the salt sea and the running water, for the everlasting hills, for the trees, and for the grass under our feet. We thank thee for our senses by which we can see the splendour of the morning, and hear the jubilant songs of love, and smell the breath of the springtime. Grant us, we pray thee, a heart wide open to all this joy and beauty, and save our souls from being so steeped in care or so darkened by passion that we pass heedless and unseeing when even the thornbush by the wayside is aflame with the glory of God.

Enlarge within us the sense of fellowship with all the living things, our litter brothers, to whom thou hast given this earth as their home in common with us. We remember with shame that in the past we have exercised the high dominion of man with ruthless cruelty, so that the voice of the Earth, which should have gone up to thee in song, has been a groan of travail. May we realize that they live, not for us alone, but for themselves and for thee, and that they love the sweetness of life, even as we, and serve thee in their place better than we in ours.

When our use of this world is over and we make for others, may we not leave anything ravished by our greed or spoiled by our ignorance, but may we hand on our common heritage fairer and sweeter through our use of it, undiminished in fertility and joy, that so our bodies may return in peace to the great mother who nourished them and our spirits may round the circle of a perfect life in thee.

Walter Rauschenbusch

The
person of Jesus

O Lord Jesus, I will embrace you who became a little child for me. In my weakness I clasp you who became weak for me. A mere man, I embrace you who is God of man. You became a man as poor as I am, and you rode into Jerusalem seated on a humble donkey. I embrace you, O Lord, because your lowliness is my greatness, your weakness is my strength, your foolishness is my wisdom.

Aelred of Rievaulx

I kiss your feet, dear Jesus, I press my lips to them, because despite my many sins, despite the burden of guilt upon me, despite my lack of judgement, I know that I have nothing to fear from you. I embrace your feet, Lord Jesus; I anoint them with the oil of my repentance. As I crouch at your feet, I know that I am safe, because you despise no one, repel no one, welcome everyone, admit everyone.

Aelred of Rievaulx

Dear Lord Jesus, the fragrance of your love draws me towards you, like the perfume of the beloved attracts the lover. I shall follow you, Lord, walking with you over beautiful hills covered with sweet-smelling wild flowers. And I will not desert you when you walk to Calvary. I shall stay beside you, and follow your body when it is taken to the tomb. Let my flesh be buried with you in that tomb, because I no longer wish to live for myself, but to rise with you into the fullness of your love.

Aelred of Rievaulx

You who bridles untamed colts
Who gives flight to birds
Who steers ships along their course,
Tame our wild hearts
Lift our souls to you,
Steer us towards the safe harbour of your
   love.

King of the saints,
Invincible Lord of the Father,
Prince of wisdom,
Source of joy,
Saviour of our race,
Cultivator of all life,

Guardian of our desires,
Whose sure hands guide us to heaven.

Fisher of men,
You cast out the sweet bait of your gospel,
You draw us out of the waters of sin,
Shepherd of men,
You call us with your sweet, gentle voice,
You invite us into your eternal sheepfold.

Clement of Alexandria

Most high, glorious God, enlighten the
darkness of my heart. And give me, Lord, a
correct faith, a sure hope, a perfect love, that
I may carry out your holy and true
commands.

St Francis of Assisi

Most powerful, most high, most holy, most
supreme Lord, you alone are good, and all
goodness comes from you. May we give you
all praise, all glory, all blessing and all honour. And may we offer back to you all the
good things which you have granted to us.

St Francis of Assisi

Who is like you,
Jesus, sweet Jesus?
You are the light of those that are spiritually
  lost.
You are the life of those that are spiritually
  dead.
You are the liberation of those that are
  imprisoned by guilt.
You are the glory of those who hate
  themselves.
You are the guardian of those who are
  paralysed by fear.
You are the guide of those who are
  bewildered by falsehood.

You are the peace of those who are in turmoil.
You are the prince of those who yearn to be
  led.
You are the priest of those who seek the
  truth.

Johann Freylinghausen

Master, Master Lover,
The Princess awaits your coming in her
  fragrant chamber,
And the married unmarried woman in her
  cage;

The harlot who seeks bread in the streets of
  her shame,
And the nun in her cloister who has no
  husband,
The childless woman too at her window,
Where frost designs the forest on the pane,
She finds you in that symmetry,
And she would mother you, and be
  comforted.

Kahlil Gibran

Master, Master Poet, Master of our silent
  desires,
The heart of the world quivers with the
  throbbing of your heart,
But it burns not with your song.
The world sits listening to your voice in
  tranquil delight,
But it rises not from its seat
To scale the ridges of your hills.
Man would dream your dream, but he
  would not wake to your dawn,
Which is his greater dream.
He would see with your vision,
But he would not drag his heavy feet to your
  throne;

Yet many have been enthroned in your name
And mitred with your power,
And have turned your golden visit
Into crowns for their head and sceptres of
  their hand.
                              Kahlil Gibran

Jesus Christ, the love that gives love,
You are higher than the highest star;
You are deeper than the deepest sea;
You cherish us as your own family;
You embrace us as your own spouse;
You rule over us as your own subjects;
You welcome us as your dearest friend.
Let all the world worship you.
                              Hildegard of Bingen

The birds have their nests and the foxes their
holes. But you were homeless, Lord Jesus,
with nowhere to rest your head. And yet
you were a hiding place where the sinner
could flee. Today you are still such a hiding
place, and I flee to you. I hide myself under
your wings, and your wings cover the
multitude of my sins.
                              Søren Kierkegaard

Jesus, when I am with you, I burn with joy.
And when the heat of love surges within my
  breast,
I want to embrace you, to clasp you to
  myself.
Yet, my beloved, my love is frustrated
By a strange, invisible barrier
That seems to stand between me and you.
If only you would break down that barrier.
And so let me rush to your arms.
I can see you clearly,
And I beg you to allow me to come to you.
I am in prison, beating my fists against the
  wall
That divides me from you.
But in the meantime I can sing your praises,
And in prayer I can speak with you.
So I will enjoy such blessings for the present,
In the hope of being united fully in the
  future.

Richard Rolle

Lord, grant me a simple, kind, open,
believing, loving and generous heart,
worthy of being your dwelling-place.

John Sergieff

Lord Christ, if we had faith
that could move mountains
yet without living charity,
What would we be?
You love us.
Without your Holy Spirit
who lives in our hearts,
what would we be?
You love us.
Taking everything on you,
you open for us a way towards faith,
towards trust in God,
who wants neither suffering
nor human distress.
Spirit of the Risen Christ,
Spirit of compassion,
Spirit of praise,
your love for each one of us
will never go away.

Roger Schutz

Lord, I am your ship.
Fill me with the gifts of your Holy Spirit.
Without you I am empty of every blessing,
And full of every sin.

Lord, I am your ship.
Fill me with the cargo of good works.
Without you I am empty of every joy,
And full of vain pleasures.

Lord, I am your ship.
Fill me with love for you.

John Sergieff

Although within us there are wounds,
Lord Christ, above all there is
the miracle of your mysterious presence.
Thus, made lighter or even set free,
we are going with you, the Christ,
from one discovery to another.

Roger Schutz

Lord, you are like a wild flower. You spring
up in places where we least expect you. The
bright colour of your grace dazzles us. When
we reach down to pluck you, hoping to
possess you for our own, you blow away in
the wind. And if we tried to destroy you, by
stamping on you and kicking you, you
would come back to life. Lord, may we come
to expect you anywhere and everywhere.
May we rejoice in your beauty. Far from

trying to possess you, may you possess us.
And may you forgive us for all the times
when we have sinned against you.

Henry Suso

Your love, Jesus, is an ocean with no shore to
bound it. And if I plunge into it, I carry with
me all the possessions I have. You know,
Lord, what these possessions are – the souls
you have seen fit to link with mine.

Thérèse of Lisieux

My God, you know that the only thing I've
ever wanted is to love you. I have no
ambition for any other glory except that. In
my childhood your love was there waiting
for me. As I grew up, it grew with me. and
now it is like a great chasm too deep to be
plumbed. Love creates love. And my love
for you, Jesus, wants to grow and expand
until it fills that chasm which you have made
for it. But it's no good. In truth my love is
less than a drop of dew lost in the ocean.
Can I love you as much as you love me? The
only way to do that is to come to you for the
loan of your own love; I could not content

myself with anything less.

Dear Jesus, I can have no certainty about this, but I do not see how you could have squandered more love on a human soul than you have on mine. That is why I venture to ask that the souls which you have entrusted to me, that I might pray for them, may experience your love as I have. One day, perhaps, in heaven I shall find out that you love them better than me. and I shall be glad of that – glad to think that these people earned your love better than I ever did. But here on earth I cannot imagine a greater wealth of love than the love you have squandered on me, without my doing anything to earn it.

Thérèse of Lisieux

Let the same mind that is in me be in Christ Jesus. For he that is not led by the spirit of Christ is none of his. Holy Jesus I admire thy love unto me also. O that I could see it through all those wounds! O that I could feel it in those stripes! O that I could hear it in all those groans! O that I could taste it beneath the gall and vinegar! O that I could

smell the savour of thy sweet ointments,
even in this Golgotha, or place of a skull. I
pray thee teach me first thy love unto me,
and then unto mankind! But in thy love
unto mankind I am beloved.

Thomas Traherne

Jesu, Lover of my soul,
    Let me to my bosom fly,
While the nearer waters roll,
    While the tempest still is high:
Hide me, O my Saviour, hide,
    Till the storm of life be past!
Safe into the haven guide,
    O, receive my soul at last!

Other refuge Have I none,
    Hangs my helpless soul on thee;
Leave, ah! leave me not alone,
    Still support and comfort me:
All my trust on thee is stayed,
    All my help from thee I bring;
Cover my defenceless head
    With the shadow of thy wing.

Thou, O Christ, art all I want,
　More than all in thee I find!
Raise the fallen, cheer the faint,
　Heal the sick, and lead the blind:
Just and holy is thy name,
　I am all unrighteousness;
False and full of sin I am
　Thou art full of truth and grace.

Plenteous grace with thee is found,
　Grace to cover all my sin;
Let the healing streams abound;
　Make and keep me pure within:
Thou of life the fountain art,
　Freely let me take of thee,
Spring thou up within my heart,
　Rise to all eternity.

Charles Wesley

O thou who camest from above
　The pure celestial fire t'impart,
Kindle a flame of sacred love
　On the mean altar of my heart!

Then let it for thy glory burn
  With inextinguishable blaze,
And tremble to its source return
  In humble love, and fervent praise.

Jesu, confirm my hearts desire
  To work, and speak, and think of thee;
Still let me guard the holy fire,
  And still stir up thy gift in me;

Ready for all thy perfect will,
  My acts of faith and love repeat,
Till death thy endless mercies seal
  And make the sacrifice complete.

Charles Wesley

Adam of St Victor died c. 1177
A canon in the abbey of St Victor in Paris,
Adam became famous for composing a large
number of sequences, rhythmical verses to be
sung at major festivals. They are often in the
form of prayers directed at Jesus.

Aelred of Rievaulx c. 1110–1167
Originally from the royal court of Scotland,
Aelred was attracted to the austerity of the
Cistercian abbey at Rievaulx. He joined in
1134, and was later made abbot. He was
loved for the gentleness of his nature, and he
recognised that close friendships between
the monks could be a precious element in
achieving intimacy with Jesus.

Alcuin of York c. 735–804
After teaching at the cathedral school of
York, Alcuin became religious adviser to
Charlemagne, and later abbot of Tours.
There he composed many prayers, both
intimate and formal, which for many
centuries were popular in public worship.

Ambrose of Milan c. 339–397

Formerly governor of Milan, Ambrose was
elected bishop by popular acclaim shortly
after his conversion to Christianity. He became a brilliant preacher and writer. Many
of his writings contain intimate prayers.

Lancelot Andrewes 1555–1626

One of the main translators of the
Authorised Version of the Bible, he was
Bishop of Ely and then Winchester. He
composed many prayers, including a book
of private devotions and a horology to be
said at each hour. It is said that he spent five
hours each day in prayer, including twice-
daily confession, profession of faith,
intercession and thanksgiving.

Anselm of Canterbury c. 1033–1109

Anselm was a monk at Bec in Normandy, where
his personality attracted many to come to him
for spiritual advice. He composed many meditations for people to use privately, in which the
whole range of human emotions are laid before
God. William I, the Conqueror, summoned
Anselm to be Archbishop of Canterbury in 1093.

George Appleton 1902–
An Anglican priest in London, Burma and India,
George became Archbishop of Western
Australia in 1963, and five years later Anglican
Archbishop of Jerusalem, where he sought to
build bridges between the different religious
communities. His numerous prayers touch on
the deepest human feelings.

Thomas Aquinas c. 1225–1274
The most influential theologian of the medieval
period, he saw theology as valueless compared
to prayer. He was a member of the Dominican
order and spent most of his life teaching in
Paris. His prayers are scattered throughout his
work, especially in the biblical commentaries.

Arjuna c. 8th century BC
Arjuna, the son of a king of northern India,
was a mighty warrior. He appears in the
Mahabharata, a great epic poem. His
conversation with Krishna, an incarnation of
God, forms a group of prayers known as the
Bhagavad Gita.

Augustine of Hippo 354–430
Augustine was a philosopher who at first
rejected Christianity, despising it as too
simple. After his eventual conversion he
became a bishop in his native North Africa,
and a prolific theologian. His ideal deeply
influenced the Protestant Reformation.

Aztec c. 15th century AD
Before the arrival of the Spanish conquerors,
the Aztec people were a great civilization,
centred upon their religion. They
worshipped the sun as a symbol of a
Supreme Deity, and believed in divine
guidance over every aspect of their lives.

John Baillie 1886–1960
John was a theological teacher and writer,
and served as President of the World
Council of Churches, believing strongly in
close relations between all Christian
denominations. Of his many writings, *A
Diary of Private Prayer* (1936) is the most
popular.

William Barclay 1907–1978
After thirteen years as a minister of a poor
industrial parish on Clydeside, in 1946
William went to teach Biblical Studies at
Glasgow University. There is a profound
simplicity in his commentaries and prayers
which has won him readers throughout the
world.

Karl Barth 1886–1968
A prominent Protestant theologian, most of
Karl's life was devoted to academic work
and to resisting the Nazi movement. His old
age was spent in prison (?) in his native
Switzerland where he composed a series of
sermons and prayers.

Basil of Caesarea c. 330–379
Basil was an educated man who gave up a
successful career to become a hermit. Others
joined him and the monastic rule he
composed remains the basis of religious life
in the Eastern Church. He was later bishop of
Caesarea, and a pious and wise defender of
the church. His many compositions include
several vivid personal prayers.

Richard Baxter 1615–1691
A strict Puritan, Richard's devotion to his
people while incumbent at Kidderminster
attracted a huge congregation. He admired
Cromwell, but believed the monarchy was
divinely instituted. Later in life he refused a
bishopric, and wrote a number of prayers
which are redolent of the Puritan spirit.

Bede c. 673–735
Bede was a monk at Jarrow, and the greatest
scholar of the early English Church. He
wrote a *Life of St Cuthbert*, and his *History of
the English Church* combines meticulous
historical research with gently spiritual
guidance.

Bernard of Clairvaux 1090–1153
Bernard was a leading proponent of the
Crusades and a ruthless opponent of
heretics. His forceful exterior hid a more
tranquil, mystical spirit within, and he wrote
popular sermons and prayers. His life
formed an inspiration for the Cistercian
order of monks.

Jacob Boehme 1575–1624
A shoemaker in Germany, Jacob rebelled
against the strictness and formality of the
Lutheran Church. His fervent writings
helped to inspire the Evangelical revival in
Britain, and appealed to philosophers such
as Newton and Hegel. He composed a set of
personal prayers for use throughout the day.

Bonaventura 1217–1274
Bonaventura was a leader of the Franciscans
after the death of Francis, and gave
theological form to many of Francis'
teachings. He shared his founder's warm,
intimate love of Jesus, and in his prayers
expressed a Christian life reflecting the
passion and resurrection of Christ.

Dietrich Bonhoeffer 1906–1945
A German Lutheran pastor, Bonhoeffer
publicly opposed the Nazi movement.
Implicated in a plot against Hitler, he was
imprisoned and executed. While in prison,
he composed a number of prayers which
express both his bitter anguish and his
unquenchable faith.

The Book of Common Prayer 1549
Thomas Cranmer drew on sources from both
the Eastern and Western Churches for this
enduring prayer book, which has nourished
English-speaking Christians for over four
centuries. In addition to the prayers in the
regular services, Cranmer wrote collects for
every Sunday of the year. Until the 1960s the
Book of Common Prayer was the official
prayer book for the whole Anglican
communion, and is still widely used today.

John Calvin 1509–1564
John Calvin inspired the Protestant
Reformation in Geneva and influenced other
countries, such as Holland and Scotland. His
daily prayers, composed for the ordinary
people of Geneva, reflect his conviction that
spiritual faith is worthless without practical
application.

Helder Camara 1909–
A Roman Catholic priest, he served as
Archbishop of Olinda and Recife, the
poorest and least developed parts of Brazil.

His collection of meditations *Into Your Hands, Lord*, expresses his unconditional love for the weak and vulnerable in his ministry.

Elizabeth Catez 1880–1906
As a teenager Elizabeth tried to live like a nun, then at the age of 21 she joined a Carmelite community near Dijon, France. She believed that the total devotion to Christ that a nun could enjoy would radiate love into the world, giving light to dark and lonely lives.

Catherine of Genoa 1447–1510
Of an aristocratic background, after her conversion to Christianity, Catherine devoted herself to nursing in a local hospital. Her wards soon became famous for their cleanliness and the cheerfulness of staff and patients alike. Her prayers reveal a soul whose faith is mixed with deep anguish.

Catherine of Siena c. 1347–1380
Catherine devoted her life entirely to Christ, and her teaching and wise counsel inspired a

close circle of friends and disciples. She wrote *The Dialogue*, a conversation between God and herself, where her own words are charged with emotional and intellectual power.

Jean-Pierre de Caussade 1675–1751
A Jesuit priest, Jean-Pierre was the author of *Self Abandonment to Divine Providence*, now ranked among the greatest spiritual classics. He taught that God is present everywhere, and that we must submit ourselves perpetually to his will.

Celtic Prayers c. 450–c. 700
After the fall of the Roman Empire, an indigenous form of Christianity developed in the British Isles, which celebrated the divine spirit in all living creatures and plants as well as the human soul. The word was spread by pilgrims, who travelled to remote regions. Although few of the surviving prayers have definite authorship, some have been attributed to Brendan, Kevin and Patrick.

Clement of Alexandria c. 150–c. 215
A distinguished scholar, well-versed in both
Greek philosophy and the Bible, he ran a
school for well-educated pagan young men
who wished to learn about Christianity. He
spoke of Christ as 'the divine tutor'.

Columbanus c. 543–c. 615
Originally from Ireland, Columbanus set up
two monasteries in heathen areas of Gaul,
where he evangelized to local people. He
then moved to Bobbio in Italy, where his
monastery became a centre of learning. He
composed one of the earliest books of
private prayer.

John Cosin 1594–1672
His *Collection of Private Devotions* was
popular amongst those who wanted a
formal discipline of personal prayer. In
addition to daily worship, he offered a series
of prayers to be said as appropriate through
the day.

Richard Crashaw 1613–1649
The son of a Puritan preacher, he came
under High Church influence, and finally
joined the Roman Catholic Church. His
poetry is profoundly influenced by the
passionate mysticism of Teresa of Avila.

Cyprian of Carthage died 258
At the height of a brilliant political career he
underwent a conversion to Christianity and
was elected Bishop of Carthage. He
composed prayers to improve public
worship in his diocese, and died a martyr
after a series of horrific persecutions.

The Didache 2nd century AD
It is probably Syrian in origin, and contains
the earliest eucharistic prayers which still
survive.

Dimma 7th century AD
Apart from the fact that he lived in the
seventh century, nothing is known of this
Irish monk. His prayers were incorporated
into many early Irish liturgies.

Dinka
A Nilotic people of southern Sudan, the
Dinka have always believed in a single God
who rules the universe. Now predominantly
Christian, they have incorporated many of
their ancient beliefs and prayers into their
new faith.

John Donne 1572–1631
After an unsuccessful career as a politician
and journalist, John Donne became an
Anglican clergyman, and later Dean of St
Paul's. More famous for his poetry, written
during his troubled middle years, he also
wrote several prayers in his more tranquil
later life.

Edmund of Abingdon c. 1180–1240
As Archbishop of Canterbury, Edmund
strived to protect the Church of England
from the greed of both king and pope.
Earlier, while he taught at Oxford, he wrote
a devotional treatise containing two simple
prayers which came to be widely used.

Erasmus 1469–1536
The most renowned scholar of his age, he
opposed both the corruption of the Catholic
church and the self-righteous zeal of many
Protestant reformers. He urged the
Protestants not to break with Rome, but his
anti-Papist satire caused the pope to ban his
works. In his prayers his sharp intellect gives
way to a soft, faithful heart.

The Exeter Book c. 950
This collection of prayers of unknown
authorship offers a unique insight into the
Anglo-Saxon religious spirit. It was given by
Leofric, Bishop of Exeter, to his cathedral,
where the manuscript was preserved.

Fenelon c. 1651–1715
In an age which emphasized human
rationality, Fenelon believed that our
relationship with God must be based on
spiritual love with no personal reward. Such
love depends entirely on God's grace,
received into inner quietness of the soul.

Charles de Foucauld 1858–1916
A French aristocrat by birth, de Foucauld
lived as a hermit in Algeria following his
conversion to Christianity. His spiritual
writings take the form of passionate
outpourings, in which he bares his soul to
God. He was revered by the desert people
but was murdered by a tribesman jealous of
his influence with them.

Francis of Assisi 1182–1226
The son of a wealthy merchant, Francis
embraced total poverty in imitation of Jesus,
and devoted himself to preaching the gospel.
Others were inspired by his gentle love and
radiant joy and eventually they formed
themselves into the Franciscan Order. His
most famous prayer, *Brother Sun, Sister
Moon*, expresses his devotion to all God's
creation.

Francis of Sales 1567–1622
One of the leaders of the Counter
Reformation in the Roman Catholic Church,
Francis' particular concern was the renewal
of spiritual discipline amongst the laity, for

whom he wrote a series of meditations on
the human condition, as well as prayers
which elucidate the basic aspects of God's
relationship with man.

Johann Freylinghausen 1670–1739
His *Spiritual Songbook* provided the popular
music of the German Pietist movement,
which urged people to enter into a personal
relationship with Jesus as their saviour. The
words of his hymns are mostly directed to
Jesus, and are charged with the passion of a
lover for the beloved.

Fulbert of Chartres c. 970–1028
As Bishop of Chartres he was renowned for
his witty sermons and philosophical
argument. Often outwardly proud and
haughty, his private prayers show his
consciousness of his own lowly origins and
the transience of worldly success.

Gemma Galgani 1878–1903
Her short life was plagued by illness, and
through prayer she acquired a profound

spiritual tranquillity which transcended the most severe physical pain. The simplicity of her writings, and her joyful sharing of the peace she received, brought her great popularity in her native Italy.

The Gelasian Sacramentary c. 500
This is the oldest official prayerbook of the Western Church. Partly composed by Gelasius, pope in 492, it also contains prayers from Gaul and Britain. It contains a series of collects for major festivals, many of them adapted for use in altar prayer books, including the Book of Common Prayer.

Kahlil Gibran 1883–1931
One of the most famous religious poets of the twentieth century, his most popular work, *The Prophet*, has been translated into over twenty languages. His imagination spread far beyond the confines of any particular religious tradition.

Gilbert of Hoyland d.1170
Abbot of the Cistercian monastery at

Swineshead in Lincolnshire, Gilbert wrote a
series of treatises, epistles and sermons
inspired by St. Bernard of Clairvaux. Most of
his work seems turgid to the modern reader,
but occasionally there is a vivid freshness to
his words.

Elizabeth Goudge 1900–1984
The daughter of an Anglican clergyman, she
became a popular novelist, displaying in her
books both a deep compassion for human
suffering and unshakeable faith in the power
of good over evil. This same compassion and
faith is expressed in her *Diary of Prayer*.

Gregory of Nazianzus 329–389
Gregory pioneered a more personal and
intimate style of prayer. Until his time
prayers had tended to be formal and
scriptural, composed for public worship. He,
however, wrote prayers for private use,
through which the individual can express
their deepest feelings to God.

Guigo the Carthusian d.1188
As superior of the Carthusian order, he saw

his main task as encouraging mystic prayer amongst his monks. He saw prayer as a means by which material things become windows into God. His prayers are filled with metaphors, bringing together the material and spiritual realms.

Joseph Hall 1574–1656
Although a bishop and royalist, Joseph was a Puritan in his beliefs and austere life. He wrote *The Art of Divine Living* in which he taught that true Puritans had much to learn from the monastic and mystic approach to spirituality. His own prayers, although Puritan, could easily have been written by a medieval mystic.

Dag Hammarskjöld 1905–1961
While Secretary-General of the United Nations, Dag gave the impression of being an agnostic humanist, but after his death the publication of his private papers showed a man deeply influenced by Christian mystics. His manuscript *Markings* shows the naked honesty of someone confronting their Maker.

George Herbert 1593–1633
His flamboyant political career ended when
the king turned against him, and he became
a country parson. His religious poems date
from immediately after this time and show
in vivid imagery both his joy and his
anguish.

Hildegard of Bingen 1098–1179
Hildegard saw visions even as a child, and
rose to become Abbess of Bingen. Her most
famous work, *Scivias*, is a series of visions,
where she acknowledges to God her own
spiritual failures and begs for his help. She
also wrote some songs in happier mood,
which she herself set to music.

Hippolytus c. 190–c. 236
He was a priest in Rome, but died in
Sardinia after a persecution. His eucharistic
prayers, *The Apostolic Tradition*, have
profoundly influenced twentieth century
liturgical writers of both the Roman Catholic
and Anglican Churches.

Henry Scott Holland 1847–1918
A canon at St Paul's Cathedral and later
Professor of Divinity at Oxford University,
he sought in his writings and sermons to
apply socialist political ideas to a Christian
morality. Yet beneath his radical thinking
was a troubled soul that sought peace and
comfort in a personal relationship with
Christ.

Gerard Manley Hopkins 1844–1889
As a Jesuit, his poetry found no favour
amongst his superiors, and he destroyed
much of what he wrote. After his death, the
emotional intensity and verbal brilliance of
the surviving poems won a wide audience.
He wrote a number of poetic prayers which
compared with his other poems have an
innocent simplicity.

Ignatius of Loyola c. 1491–1556
After a career as a soldier, Ignatius became a
Christian and began to compose *The Spiritual
Exercises* – a series of meditations designed
to lead souls as soldiers of Christ. In 1538 he
and some friends formed the Society of Jesus

– the Jesuits – which took the *Spiritual Exercises* as their basis.

Philip Jebb 1932–
A monk at Downside, where he eventually became Head of the school, he experienced as a novice a severe breakdown. During this time he found relief in composing prayers in which he struggles to relate his faith to his suffering.

John of the Cross 1542–1591
After meeting Teresa of Avila, John tried to reform the Carmelite order from within, but met with strong opposition. While in prison in Toledo he wrote a number of poetic prayers and prose works, regarded as amongst the finest mystical works ever written.

Samuel Johnson 1709–1784
Famous for compiling the first English dictionary, Samuel's personal life was often dissolute and chaotic, although he expressed higher aspirations through the majestic prose of his prayers. Some of his prayers were written in response to the death of his wife.

Ben Jonson 1573–1637
As an actor, he killed a fellow actor in a duel, and while in prison wrote his first major play. In his day his plays were compared with those of Shakespeare. Amongst his poems are two prayers of repentance.

Margery Kempe c. 1373–c. 1432
Despite psychological turmoil, Margery was a devout Christian. She travelled Europe seeking spiritual enlightenment and learned to see Christ in ordinary people. She devoted her old age to nursing her invalid husband, and dictating the first autobiography to be written in English, she herself being illiterate.

Thomas Ken 1637–1711
As a bishop, Thomas wrote a method of daily prayer for ordinary people, consisting of a series of short 'ejaculations' to be learned by heart and spoken at appropriate moments during the day. He also wrote several hymns which remain popular.

Søren Kierkegaard 1813–1855
His philosophical writings, regarded as the
origin of modern existentialism, rose out of
his own spiritual crisis. He regarded
subjective experience as the only source of
truth. To him Jesus was not a historical
figure, but a contemporary spiritual figure
with whom he could communicate directly.

John Knox c. 1513–1572
Greatly influenced by Calvin's rule in
Geneva, he became leader of the Scottish
Reformation, inspiring people with his fiery
preaching and personal holiness. He taught
that each activity of the day should begin
with prayer seeking God's blessing.

William Laud 1573–1645
A fervent opponent of the Puritans, he
sought to restore the colour and ritual of
medieval worship to the Anglican church.
As Archbishop of Canterbury under King
Charles I, he used increasingly forceful
means to impose his ideas. But during the
Civil War the Parliamentary forces
imprisoned and executed him.

Brother Lawrence 1611–1691
After serving in the French army he joined a
Carmelite monastery. After his death, letters
and notes found in his cell were published,
along with many of his sayings. In his
writings there are two short prayers which
summarize his spirituality.

George MacDonald 1824–1905
Originally a minister in Aberdeen, he was
dismissed for suspected heresy, and became
a writer of children's fiction. Recently his
religious works have won greater attention,
particularly *Unspoken Sermons* which
presents the Christian faith with humour
and imagination.

George Macleod 1895–1991
A Church of Scotland minister, Macleod
founded the Iona Community in 1938, based
on the island from which St Columba
evangelised Scotland. Many were inspired by
his religious and social ideals and met each
summer on the island to pray and to discuss
how to transform society. His robust prayers,
while rooted in the concerns of his time, are

universal in their application, since he sees
God in all social situations and in all living
creatures.

Frederick Macnutt 1873–1949
As an army chaplain he began to compose
prayers in the First World War and continued throughout his ministry, publishing
them all in a *Prayer Manual*. In form and
style the prayers follow the Anglican collect,
but the substance is fresh and sharp.

Mahayana Buddhism c. 7th century AD
Early Buddhism had no belief in a supreme
deity. But as the religion spread northwards,
through Tibet and into China, more theistic
ideas were added. These included the notion
of God coming down to earth, and the hope
of being reborn with God in eternal paradise.

Mechthild of Magdeburg c. 1210–c. 1280
A member of the Béguine community, she
lived under rigorous austerities. Her book,
The Flowing Light of Godhead, is a collection of
spiritual songs and moral reflections, in the
form of poetic prayers.

Thomas Merton 1915–1968
A convert to Roman Catholicism in his twenties, Merton entered a Trappist monastery in Kentucky. Initially, his faith was narrow and rigid, but his experiences of monastic spirituality gradually broadened his religious horizons, so that in later years he formed close contacts with Buddhist and Hindu monks.

Eric Milner-White 1884–1963
A founder-member of the Anglican religious order of priests, the Oratory of the Good Shepherd, he became Dean of York where he gained a reputation as a composer of hymns and prayers.

Mohammed 570–632
The founder of Islam, Mohammed received a series of divine revelations while meditating on a mountain near Mecca. He continued to hear such messages for twenty years, and they were collected to form the *Koran*, Islam's sacred Scripture. It includes a number of prayers, most of which come from the mouths of the Hebrew prophets Noah, Abraham and Moses.

Mozarabic Sacramentary 3rd century AD
From the earliest times the Iberian peninsula
had its own liturgical form, which included
special prayers for the various spiritual and
moral virtues. This liturgy continued to be
used through the period of Muslim rule, but
when Spain was reconquered by Christian
forces in the eleventh century, Roman rites
were imposed.

Thomas Münzer c. 1490–1525
An ordained priest and originally a follower of
Luther, he began an independent church after
falling out with Luther over baptism. For his
part in the Peasants' Revolt in Germany he
was executed. His prayers, despite his stormy
life, express his faith with succinct eloquence.

Nanak 1469–1538
The founder of the Sikh religion in north-west
India, he sought to reconcile Hinduism and
Islam, whose rivalry was causing much misery
and bloodshed. He combined the monotheism
of Islam with the tolerance and mysticism of
the Hindu tradition.

John Henry Newman 1801–1890
His stormy career in both the Roman
Catholic and Protestant churches is balanced
by his rigorous daily discipline of worship
and meditation. His striving to work out his
theology is clearly expressed in *Meditations
of Christian Doctrine*. The poetic prayer, *Lead,
Kindly Light*, is still a popular hymn.

Reinhold Niebuhr 1892–1971
Professor of Applied Christianity in New
York, in both his theology and his
spirituality his primary concern was the
relationship between the revelation of God in
the Bible and the political and social problems which beset mankind. The shadow of
world war looms over many of his prayers.

Huub Oosterhuis 1933–
A Jesuit priest, Oosterhuis' ministry has
mainly been to the student community of
Amsterdam. In his *Your Word is Near*, he
expresses through prayer his conviction that
God is active in every aspect of human life,
and that Christians must be open and
sensitive to this divine action.

Origen c. 185–c. 254
A brilliant theologian and biblical scholar,
often in conflict with the institutional church,
he taught that the Bible should be understood
on three levels: literal, Moral and allegorical.
This attitude is reflected in his short, simple
prayers.

Prayers from Papyri
Archaeological excavations have brought to
light many fragments of early Christian
writings and prayers. Precise dates are
impossible to determine, but the prayers
probably range from between the second
and fourth centuries.

Blaise Pascal 1623–1662
A mathematician and scientist, he is now
famous for his religious reflections. A
normally depressed person, he had an
experience of intense joy after which he
wrote down his *Memorial*, a passionate
prayer which he kept with him until his
death. Beset by ill-health he came to regard
sickness as a blessing for the closeness to
God he experienced.

Alan Paton 1903–1988
One of South Africa's foremost writers, his book, *Cry, the Beloved Country* drew him into the political struggle against racism. His religious convictions, expressed in meditations and prayers in *Instrument of Thy Peace*, taught that self-giving love, not violence, is the only valid means of political change.

Book of Psalms
Traditionally attributed to King David, the Psalms were not collected into their present form until the rebuilding of the temple in Jerusalem, where they were used as hymns. They are models of honest prayer, in that they express to God the whole range of human emotions.

E.B. Pusey 1800–1882
As a leader of the Oxford Movement, which sought to restore Catholic doctrine to the Anglican Church, his own contribution was to inspire the renewal of monastic life and the medieval traditions of spirituality. His prayers are invariably intimate and personal and to modern taste can seem sentimental.

Karl Rahner 1904–1984
A Jesuit theologian, he exerted a major
influence on the Second Vatican Council
which transformed the Roman Catholic
church. Yet while at the height of his fame
and power he wrote a prayer acknowledging
to God his ignorance in the face of the divine
mystery.

Brother Ramon 1935–
A member of the Anglican Society of St
Francis, he now lives as a hermit. He
compiled a personal retreat programme,
Heaven on Earth, based on his experience of
leading retreats. His prayers are rich in vivid
metaphors.

Walter Rauschenbusch 1861–1918
A Baptist minister and a professor of
theology who was the leading exponent of
the social gospel movement in America,
which regarded social and economic justice
as central to Christ's message. His book *For
God and People* demonstrated the spiritual
implications of the social gospel.

Richard Rolle c. 1300–1349
As a hermit on the Yorkshire moors he
experienced God as a lover, and composed
songs and prayers expressing in simple,
vivid phrases his joy. He began touring the
country, singing and praying with the
people he met. Although the church author-
ities regarded him with suspicion, he was
very popular amongst the ordinary people.

Christina Rossetti 1830–1894
An invalid for most of her life, Rossetti was a
prolific poet and lyricist, and her most
famous poem, *In the Bleak Midwinter*, is now
a popular Christmas hymn. In later life she
wrote a devotional commentary on the Book
of Revelations in which reflections on
biblical texts are interspersed with prayers.

Roger Schutz 1915–
The founder of the Taizé movement in 1944,
Brother Roger has written a large number of
prayers and meditations which express a
joyful and robust faith. The community at
Taizé has become an ecumenical focus of
spiritual renewal.

John Sergieff 1829–1908
John was a priest in a remote part of Russia.
He became renowned for his concern for the
poor, collecting huge sums of money for
their support, and for the prayers he
composed which ordinary people could
adapt and use for themselves.

Simeon the Theodidact c. 949–c. 1022
Abbot of a monastery in Constantinople, he
taught that all Christians could experience
direct communion with God, without the
need for priests. This antagonised church
leaders and he was exiled to a remote region,
where he died. His two most famous prayers
express his desire to see God, and then his
first direct encounter with God.

Johann Starck 1680–1756
A leading member of the German Pietist
movement, he wrote many prayers and
hymns. His book, *A Daily Handbook for Days of
Joy and Sorrow*, was popular throughout
Germany for about two hundred years. It
contained prayers for every situation as well
as a weekly pattern of devotion.

Robert Louis Stevenson 1850–1894
At the age of thirty-eight he went with his
wife to live in Samoa. He was already a
famous novelist, and among the Samoans he
soon gained the reputation as a 'Tusitala', or
'storyteller'. He also composed prayers to be
said each evening in his household.

Henry Suso *c.* 1295–1366
While a Dominican friar, Suso suffered
greatly from depression during which
prayer became a meaningless ritual.
However, an intense mystical experience
brought him into close proximity with God
with whom he now felt able to
communicate. His spiritual autobiography
records his dialogue with God, both in joy
and sadness.

Rabindranath Tagore 1861–1941
A Bengali poet and mystic, he sought to
combine the best in Western and Hindu
traditions. He translated his most famous
collection of spiritual verses, *Gitanjali*, into
English and won the Nobel Prize for
Literature.

Jeremy Taylor 1613–1667
At first royal chaplain to King Charles I and then
after the Civil War domestic chaplain in a small
country house, his extravagant tastes gradually
gave way to a deep mystical awareness of God's
presence. He wrote a pattern of prayer for
ordinary people to discern God in all things.

Teilhard de Chardin 1881–1955
A French Jesuit theologian and palaeon-
tologist, he formed a cosmic vision which
combined science and religion. In *The Divine
Milieu* he reflects on the forces which attract
the soul to and repel it from, God. In *The
Cosmic Life* he perceives God as the utmost
fulfilment of the evolutionary process.

Teresa of Avila 1515–1582
A member of a Carmelite order, after a series
of ecstatic experiences she combined an
intense spiritual life with tireless administra-
tive activity, founding with John of the Cross
a new and primitive rule of Carmelites. She
composed a number of poetic prayers,
including the *Book of God's Mercies*.

Mother Teresa 1910–
For twenty years Teresa taught in a convent school in India but in 1948 left it to work amongst the sick and the dying in the slums of Calcutta. She founded the Missionaries of Charity, which now has over two hundred branches worldwide. Her simple prayers reflect her radiant love.

Thérèse of Lisieux 1873–1897
A member of a Carmelite order, her spiritual life was so intense that her mother superior asked her to write her autobiography. Its child-like holiness which shines through has made her one of the most popular saints of all time.

Thomas à Kempis c. 1380–1471
A monk of the Brethren of common Life, he spent his life transcribing manuscripts, including an entire Bible, and writing politically. His *Meditations on the Life of Christ* is a collection of prayers arising out of his own profound reflection on the Gospels.

Thomas Traherne 1637–1674
An Anglican priest who saw the purpose of life as the attainment of holiness, and could see holiness in all living things. His most famous work, *Centuries of Meditations*, was discovered and published over two hundred years after his death. Its short reflections and prayers sparkle with hope and love.

Tychon of Zadonsk 1724–1783
A gruff and unkempt monk who preferred the company of the Russian peasants to that of priests and lords. Firmly rejecting the fashionable nationalist philosophy of the West, he believed that prayer should be the basis of all thought and action.

Manikka Vasahar 8th century AD
He was chief minister of Southern India, renowned for his gentleness. His famous prayers, still used among Tamil-speaking people, were uttered on a visit to the temple at Perundurai when he was suddenly seized by an intense religious emotion.

Atharva Veda c. 1500 BC
The most ancient sacred texts of Hinduism, the
'Vedas' are a collection of hymns, originally
oral, but eventually written down. The fourth
veda, the Atharva Veda, includes a number of
prayers. Although many deities are mentioned
in the Vedas, these prayers suggest a belief in a
single, supreme power.

Jean-Baptiste Marie Vianney 1786–1859
Popularly known as Curé d'Ars, he served
that parish for over forty years. His reputation as a confessor and spiritual director
drew people from throughout France.

Wapokomo
This tribe, who inhabit land to the west of
Lake Tana, never succumbed to the power
and faith of the Christian Ethiopians to their
east. But, as their prayers illustrate, they were
deeply influenced by the Christian spirit.

Charles Wesley 1707–1788
The younger brother of the founder of the
Methodist movement, Wesley wrote hymns

to be sung at open air evangelical meetings to the popular tunes of the day. Their simple, memorable phrases, and their pleasing rhymes and rhythms have made his hymns vehicles by which all Christians can express their love of God.

William of St Thierry c. 1065–1148
As first abbot of the Benedictine abbey of St Thierry, he founded in 1135 a Cistercian house in the Ardennes, influenced by St Bernard of Clairvaux. Like Bernard he engaged passionately in the theological controversies of the day, but his lasting reputation rests on his spiritual works, *The Golden Epistle* and *On Contemplating God*.

Count von Zinzendorf 1700–1760
The founder of the Moravian church, he earned the suspicion of the Lutheran church which mistrusted his enthusiastic personal relationship with God. His writings had a profound influence on the Evangelical revival.

Zoroaster 6th century BC
Little is known about Zoroaster himself, but
his Persian religion had a profound
influence on Jewish and Christian thought.
He taught people to worship a single God,
praying directly to him and obeying his
moral laws. Zoroaster saw himself as a
reformer bringing together the wisdom of all
the ancient religions.

COLLINS GEM

COLLINS GEM

Bestselling Collins Gem titles include:

Gem English Dictionary (£3.50)
Gem Calorie Counter (£2.99)
Gem Thesaurus (£2.99)
Gem French Dictionary (£3.50)
Gem German Dictionary (£3.50)
Gem Basic Facts Mathematics (£2.99)
Gem Birds (£3.50)
Gem Wild Flowers (£3.50)
Gem Card Games (£3.50)
Gem World Atlas (£3.50)

All Collins Gems are available from your local bookseller or can be ordered direct from the publishers.

In the UK, contact Mail Order, Dept 2M, HarperCollins Publishers, Westerhill Rd, Bishopbriggs, Glasgow, G64 2QT, listing the titles required and enclosing a cheque or p.o. for the value of the books plus £1.00 for the first title and 25p for each additional title to cover p&p. Access and Visa cardholders can order on 041-772 2281 (24 hr).

In Australia, contact Customer Services, HarperCollins Distribution, Yarrawa Rd, Moss Vale 2577 (tel. [048] 68 0300). **In New Zealand**, contact Customer Services, HarperCollins Publishers, 31 View Rd, Glenfield, Auckland 10 (tel. [09] 444 3740). **In Canada**, contact your local bookshop.

All prices quoted are correct at time of going to press.